IMAGES
of America

CATHOLIC KANSAS CITY

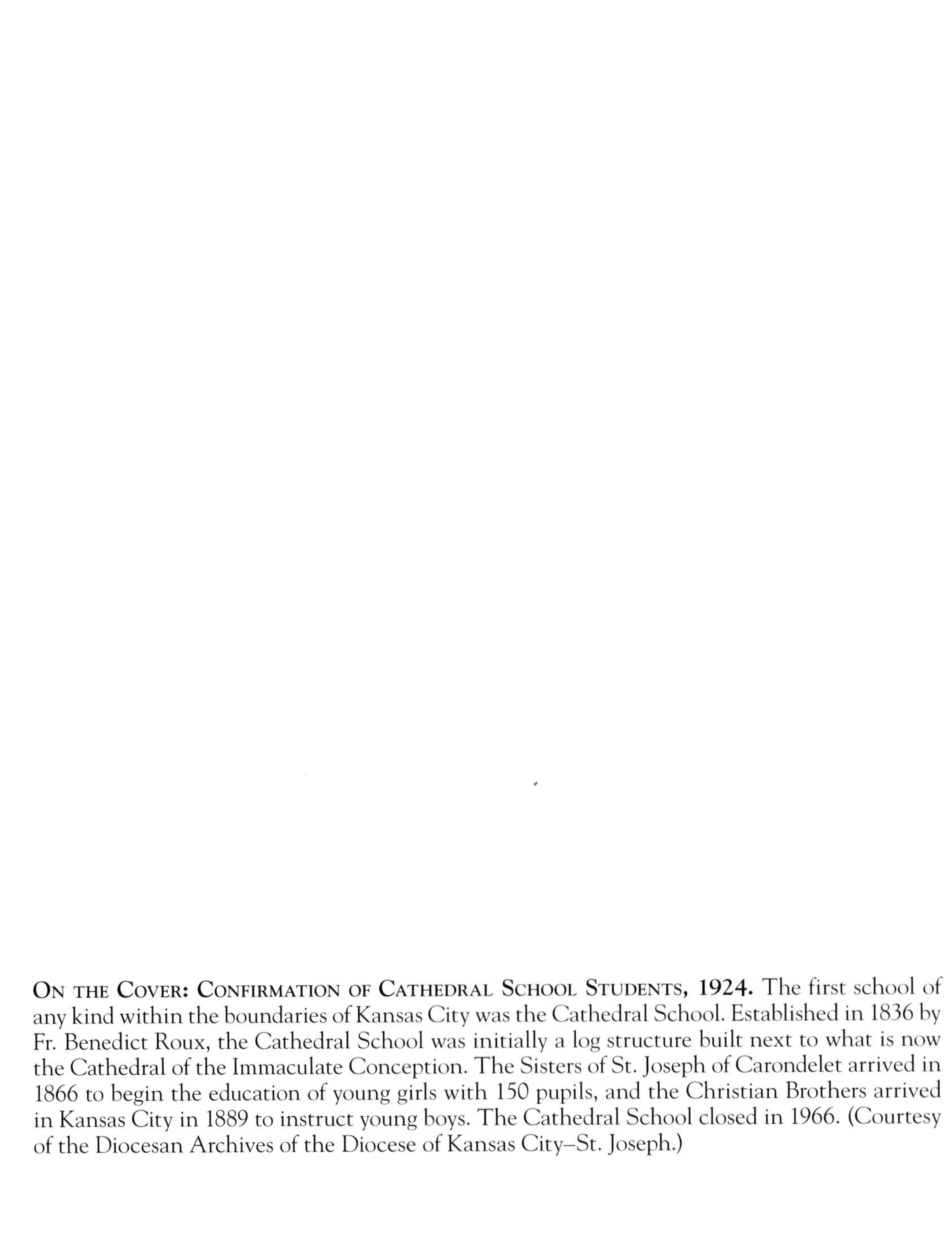

On the Cover: Confirmation of Cathedral School Students, 1924. The first school of any kind within the boundaries of Kansas City was the Cathedral School. Established in 1836 by Fr. Benedict Roux, the Cathedral School was initially a log structure built next to what is now the Cathedral of the Immaculate Conception. The Sisters of St. Joseph of Carondelet arrived in 1866 to begin the education of young girls with 150 pupils, and the Christian Brothers arrived in Kansas City in 1889 to instruct young boys. The Cathedral School closed in 1966. (Courtesy of the Diocesan Archives of the Diocese of Kansas City–St. Joseph.)

Zachary S. Daughtrey
Foreword by
Most Reverend James V. Johnston Jr.

ISBN 978-1-4671-0575-0

Published by Arcadia Publishing
Charleston, South Carolina

Printed in the United States of America

Library of Congress Control Number: 2020950134

For all general information, please contact Arcadia Publishing:
Telephone 843-853-2070
Fax 843-853-0044
E-mail sales@arcadiapublishing.com
For customer service and orders:
Toll-Free 1-888-313-2665

Visit us on the Internet at www.arcadiapublishing.com

For Charlie.

Contents

Foreword		6
Acknowledgments		7
Introduction		8
1.	Catholic Beginnings in Kansas City	9
2.	Parishes and Bishops	17
3.	Catholic Education in Kansas City	69
4.	Religious Orders and Lay Organizations	89
5.	Assisting the Community	103
6.	Ethnic and Racial Groups of Catholic Kansas City	115

FOREWORD

One of the areas of our life together that we neglect at our own peril is our history—the stories of our past. Without these reference points, we lose sight of the trajectory and meaning of essential aspects of life. Mindful of this, I commend this volume to those who seek to learn about the stories of the Catholic community in Kansas City, Missouri.

It has been said that Kansas City is the westernmost city of the eastern United States and the easternmost city of the west. In other words, its history is defined by being on the frontier. Catholics have always been in the minority in Kansas City, but their role in the cultural, political, and spiritual life of the community has been disproportionately larger than their numbers. First evangelized by Jesuit missionaries and Catholic priests on horseback, the church grew with increased immigration and the sheer growth of a nation.

As the Catholic community matured, prominent institutions in education, healthcare, and social services were established. Many of these continue to affect the city and surrounding area to the present day. More than anything, however, it is the Catholic people who have helped make Kansas City what it is today through prayer, worship, family life, service, and hard work.

I hope that those who reside in Kansas City, or who have a connection to it, will find joy in this work as it recounts the history and memories of so many who helped shape our present and prepare for our future.

I wish to thank Zachary Daughtrey, the archivist for the Diocese of Kansas City–St. Joseph, for his leadership in this endeavor. Capturing a history accurately is a detail-intensive and sometimes complex undertaking. I hope this will help us all to better understand and appreciate the important role the Catholic Church has had in Kansas City and inspire us to contribute in greater ways as we progress through the next century.

Peace,
Most Reverend James V. Johnston Jr.
Bishop of Kansas City–St. Joseph

ACKNOWLEDGMENTS

The completion of any project is not due to the author's efforts alone but rather to the collection of people who helped them throughout the process. To start, I want to thank the steadfast support of my wife, Katie; my mother, Glenna; and my aunt Tam for their support and encouragement throughout this long process. I would also like to single out my son Charlie for giving me hours of laughter and joy, which has certainly aided in keeping my spirits up while researching and writing this book.

I have also been blessed with an extraordinary staff in the diocesan archives. I would like to thank the contributions, criticisms, and inputs of Deacon Ralph Wehner and Tara Harris, who pulled photographs and provided helpful input into this venture.

A special thank-you is also merited to diocesan counselor Pat Miller and the chancellor of the Diocese of Kansas City–St. Joseph, Fr. Ken Riley, for their assistance in getting this project off the ground and supported by the diocese. Lastly, I would like to thank His Excellency Bishop James V. Johnston Jr. for his graciousness not only in writing the foreword for this book but his kind words as well.

Unless otherwise noted, all images appear courtesy of the Diocesan Archives of the Diocese of Kansas City–St. Joseph.

Introduction

The success of Catholicism in Kansas City was far from a certainty. French Catholics had been trickling into the area for several decades by the time the ever-dour Fr. Benedict Roux found himself in what he most assuredly considered the end of civilization, religious or otherwise. "I lose all hope to bring them back in the road of salvation," Father Roux complained when speaking about the Catholicism of French settlers near the Missouri River. "I have never seen so much conceitedness and presumption joined to so much ignorance about the Catholic faith." Roux had been in the region a mere few months, but apparently his mind was made up about the prospects for the future of the Catholic Church in western Missouri.

Yet during the 1840s and 1850s, two extraordinary priests—Fr. Bernard Donnelly and Fr. John J. Hogan—arrived in what became Kansas City in 1853; they would shape Catholicism in the city for centuries to come. Unlike Father Roux, Father Donnelly possessed the physical and emotional strength to will the Catholic Church to take root in the area. "I had a small trunk, a few books, and five dollars in my pocket," Donnelly reminisced years later. "I assisted at High Mass, preached the Unity of the Church after the Gospel, as also in the evening on the Catholic doctrine of Scripture interpretation." Father Donnelly had no doubts of what his mission was.

Father Hogan arrived in Kansas City in 1857 under similar circumstances and scoured the countryside for any Catholics he could find. "North Missouri was a beautiful country," remarked Hogan, "but a land unknown to the Church. . . . I would with God's help attempt to make a beginning there." Like Father Hogan, Father Donnelly traveled extensively in the Jackson County countryside ministering to all Catholics he encountered along the way. In 1865, Father Donnelly set his passions toward the establishment of permanent Catholic education in Kansas City. Writing to the Sisters of St. Joseph of Carondelet in December 1865, he requested they head to Kansas City to provide the city's Catholic children with a religious education. In 1866, the Sisters arrived and began two centuries of service and educational instruction.

Catholicism, bolstered by the influx of Irish and Germans throughout the 1860s and 1870s, finally warranted the establishment of an episcopal see in Kansas City in 1880. Father Hogan, who found continued success for the church north of the Missouri River, was chosen as the new bishop for the Diocese of Kansas City. Receiving Bishop Hogan when he arrived by train in Kansas City on September 10, 1880, was Father Donnelly. With the arrival of Bishop Hogan and the formation of Kansas City as an episcopal see, Father Donnelly retired from service. Friends and colleagues within the clergy wrote to Archbishop Peter Kenrick in St. Louis to have Donnelly elevated to monsignor. When Father Donnelly learned of this proposal, he immediately wrote to Archbishop Kenrick in protest. According to Father Donnelly, he had achieved his goal, and the church in Kansas City was on solid ground with Bishop Hogan.

In the decades since, the Catholic Church in Kansas City has experienced uncountable instances of success and failure, triumphs and tragedies. Catholics in the city have experienced sorrow as parishes, parish schools, high schools, and institutions have been shuttered. They have witnessed the turmoil of civil unrest for those fighting against racial injustices and the upheavals wrought by revolutions in Mexico, Vietnam, and Central America. Yet in the face of these seemingly insurmountable negatives, Catholics in Kansas City have overcome through prayer, hard work, and Midwestern tenacity. There are no doubts that Catholicism will continue to thrive in the area. In the words of former diocesan priest and archivist Fr. Michael Coleman, Catholics have come this far by faith. There is nothing stopping them from going a bit more.

One

Catholic Beginnings in Kansas City

The arrival of French fur trappers and traders who settled along the Missouri River in what would become Kansas City signaled the beginning of Catholicism in the region. Yet whether or not Catholicism would thrive was another story. "The truth is," lamented Fr. Benedict Roux in an 1831 letter to Bishop Joseph Rosati, the first bishop of the Diocese of St. Louis, "that the Catholics of [western Missouri] are incapable of supporting a priest decently, being so few in number." Though pessimistic in tone, Father Roux's feelings were not unfounded, as he reported only nine Catholic families in the area upon his arrival. Out of frustration and despair, Roux returned to St. Louis in 1835.

Yet despite Father Roux's disparaging words regarding the existence of Catholicism in western Missouri, Catholicism had indeed existed in the region as early as 1723. French fur traders and merchants settled along the Missouri River near present-day Kansas City at Chouteau's Bluff and established a chapel. The arrival of Catholic missionaries, most notably Fr. Bernard Donnelly in 1845, signaled the permanency and success of the church in the area. The Catholic population in the region was enough to warrant the establishment of first the Diocese of St. Joseph on March 3, 1868, and the Diocese of Kansas City on September 10, 1880, as suffragan sees from the Archdiocese of St. Louis.

EARLY KANSAS CITY WATERFRONT, 1853. Although incorporated into the state of Missouri in 1853, Kansas City had been long settled by Catholics from France who lived primarily on the waterfront near the Great Bend of the Missouri River. In 1821, Francois Gesseau Chouteau set up a permanent trading post in what he termed the "village of the Kansa" and agreed to finance the construction of a Catholic church in what is today the Quality Hill District of Kansas City. By the 1840s, Catholics from Ireland and Germany arrived in Kansas City to escape religious persecution in their native countries.

REPRODUCTION OF ST. JOHN FRANCIS REGIS CHURCH, C. 1960. Fr. Benedict Roux arrived in Kansas City in 1833 to establish a canonical parish. He purchased the original acreage to build the church at Eleventh and Pennsylvania Streets. The name given to the new parish in what ultimately became the Cathedral of the Immaculate Conception was St. John Francis Regis, which Catholics in the area used consistently by 1843. Fr. Bernard Donnelly described the log church as "rude." "The walls and flat ceiling," he noted, "were roughly plastered. In addition to the Stations of the Cross, three oil paintings hung in the church. Over the altar was a painting of the Crucifixion."

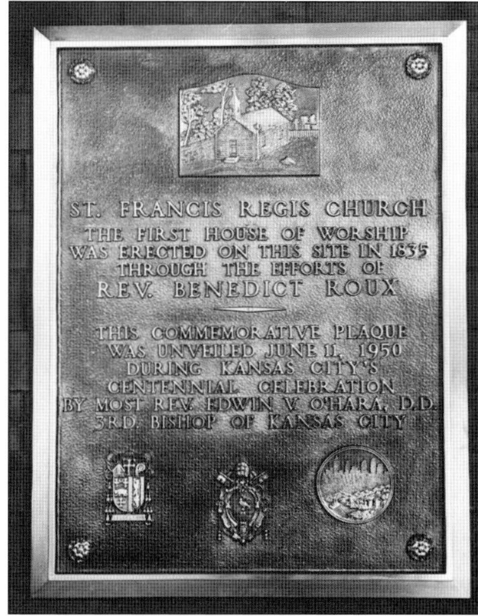

PLAQUE DEDICATED TO FR. BENEDICT ROUX, 1950. Father Roux arrived in 1833 in what would become Kansas City and found only nine Catholic families living in the entirety of western Missouri. Decidedly discouraged by the outlook of his mission, Father Roux wrote to Bishop Joseph Rosati, the first bishop of the Diocese of St. Louis, "that the Catholics of [western Missouri] are incapable of supporting a priest decently, being so few in number." Despite his misgivings, Roux nevertheless strove to create a permanent parish for the Catholic community before leaving Kansas City in 1835.

Fr. Bernard Donnelly, c. 1861. If there is any one priest to be singled out when discussing who was most instrumental in making Catholicism not only permanent but successful in Kansas City, it would be Fr. Bernard Donnelly. Born in Kilnacreeva in County Cavan, Ireland, Donnelly arrived in the United States in 1839 and Missouri in 1840. After his ordination in 1845, he taught classics and higher mathematics at St. Mary Seminary in Perry County, Missouri, before his appointment "for the Missions of Westport Landing, Independence, Westport, Liberty, Clay [County] and about a hundred other places," in his words. Donnelly helped establish St. Mary's Parish in Independence as well as the construction of the first brick cathedral in Kansas City, using bricks made from a brickyard owned and operated by Donnelly himself. Described as strong-willed and humorous, Donnelly died on December 14, 1880. He is buried in Mount St. Mary Cemetery in Kansas City.

St. Mary's Parish, Independence, 1990. Formally organized by Father Donnelly in 1845, St. Mary's Parish in Independence serves as the oldest operational parish within Kansas City. Ordered by Archbishop Peter Kenrick of St. Louis to visit the western settlements of Catholics along the Missouri River, Father Donnelly arrived on May 17, 1845. Donnelly discovered approximately 12 families of French and Native American heritage in the area. Vincentian missionary Fr. Thomas Burke, who had traveled through Independence several months earlier, bluntly notified Donnelly that "no church or . . . house [is] here for you—that's what you are sent here for, to build them." Father Donnelly lived for a short time at the home of Col. Thomas Davy, where he said Mass for local Catholics. Shortly thereafter, Davy, along with Anthony Cosgrove, William Howe, and Samuel C. Owens, as well as some non-Catholics in Independence, raised enough money for Donnelly to construct a church in 1846.

TEMPORARY CHURCH BUILDING FOR CATHEDRAL, 1857. While the original log church occupied by St. Francis Regis was torn down in favor of a new brick structure for the recently named Cathedral of the Immaculate Conception in 1857, cathedral parishioners temporarily attended Mass in this house. It was occupied by a Mrs. Brady and was on Boonville Street immediately north of the St. James Hotel. Fr. Bernard Donnelly used the lower floor of the home for Mass.

CATHEDRAL OF THE IMMACULATE CONCEPTION, 1857. As the population increased and more Catholics flowed into the area, the need for a new church became apparent. Though the old log church served the small community well for almost two decades, a larger building was necessary by the late 1850s. In 1857, a structure facing Broadway Boulevard between Eleventh and Twelfth Streets was built using bricks from Father Donnelly's brickyard. Donnelly ordered a bell from Cincinnati in 1857; upon its arrival via steamboat, it was installed on the pilaster at the southeast corner of the church. The bell was donated by Thomas Corrigan, who lived near the cathedral.

CATHEDRAL HIGH ALTAR, C. 1900. The interior of the new brick cathedral was simple yet opulent. The high altar was a plain table with pilasters and the monogram of the Blessed Mother. Shelving behind the altar held the tabernacle, crosses, candlesticks, and candelabras with crystal prisms. Behind the altar was an oil painting of the crucifixion from the log church. The sanctuary around the altar was considered miniscule even by contemporary standards, but here Father Donnelly could regularly be found praying and saying the rosary unless the weather was too cold.

Bishop John J. Hogan, 1880. Born in County Limerick, Ireland, in 1829, the energetic and strong-willed John Joseph Hogan arrived in the United States in 1848 and was ordained to the priesthood in 1852. Initially assigned to parishes outside of St. Louis, Hogan was called by Archbishop Peter Kenrick to travel to northwest Missouri with orders to minister to Catholics living throughout the region. The efforts of Father Hogan made it possible to establish a permanent see in western Missouri with the founding of the Diocese of St. Joseph in 1868, and Hogan was named bishop. When the Holy See erected another diocese comprising counties south to the Missouri-Arkansas border as well as counties south of the Missouri River, Bishop Hogan became the first bishop of the Diocese of Kansas City on September 10, 1880.

Parishioners Leaving Celebration at Cathedral, c. 1920. Major events associated with the cathedral were always cause for celebration across Kansas City. When the cornerstone for the present-day cathedral was laid on May 11, 1882, it is estimated that 10,000 witnessed the ceremony. People from as far away as Leavenworth, Kansas, and Sedalia, Missouri, were brought in by train, and various religious and civic organizations marched in a parade through the city. A sermon was given in English by the archbishop of Chicago, Patrick A. Feehan, and one was given in German by the abbot of Conception Abbey, Frowin Conrad, OSB, which highlights the ethnic diversity of Kansas City's Catholic community by the early 20th century.

Two

Parishes and Bishops

Following the establishment of St. John Francis Regis Parish, which developed over time into the Cathedral of the Immaculate Conception, parishes began to be created consistently throughout Kansas City. When Bishop John J. Hogan arrived to take charge of the Diocese of Kansas City, he inherited a vast territory stretching from the south bank of the Missouri River all the way to the Arkansas border. An estimated 30,000 Catholics were already present in the diocese, and thousands more entered Kansas City every month.

The founding of Old St. Patrick Parish at Eighth and Cherry Streets served as the catalyst for the expansion of parishes after the cathedral. The creation of SS. Peter and Paul, St. Francis Seraph, St. Joseph, Our Lady of Sorrows, and Our Lady of Perpetual Help quickly followed suit. The rapid establishment of these parishes would not have been possible without the tenacity of strong-willed diocesan leadership, however.

Since its inception, the Diocese of Kansas City, and later the Diocese of Kansas City–St. Joseph, has been blessed with a line of bishops who were forward-thinking and willing to change with the times to keep the church in Kansas City ever-evolving. Bishop Hogan provided the grit, determination, and organizational skills to keep Catholicism in Kansas City on a solid footing as it progressed into the 20th century. Bishop Thomas F. Lillis exuded the princely nature of the episcopacy and the grand vision necessary for the church's expansion, keeping pace with the city's growth. Bishop Edwin V. O'Hara built upon the foundation laid by Bishop Lillis but sought to greatly develop Catholic education within Kansas City as well as increasingly involve the laity through Catholic Action. Bishop Charles Helmsing and Bishop John Sullivan radiated the energy of the Second Vatican Council changes to the church and instituted these changes for the positive good of Catholicism in the city. Finally, Bishop Raymond Boland brought the warmth and decisiveness required to overcome the challenges the church faced heading into a new millennium.

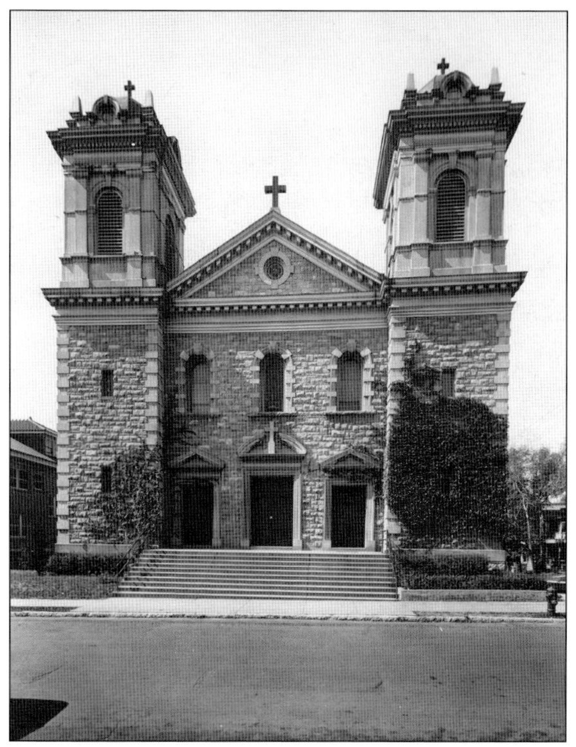

Our Lady of Good Counsel, c. 1950. Our Lady of Good Counsel Parish, originally known as the Westport Church, was established in 1871 for Catholics in the Westport neighborhood of Kansas City. Good Counsel was initially so large that 12 parishes were later carved out of its territory. Like other parishes in the area, Fr. Bernard Donnelly was instrumental in its construction and overall success. Donnelly purchased in his own name the land on which the current Good Counsel parish resides and deeded the property to the Archdiocese of St. Louis on January 16, 1873. The parish was under threat of dissolving early in its life; Donnelly consistently fought the sale of church property at county auction due to mechanics' liens against it. Yet despite its initial struggles, Good Counsel began to thrive in the late 1890s and early 1900s as immigrant families, primarily Irish, consistently flowed into the Westport area.

Mass at Our Lady of Good Counsel, 1955. As the community continued to expand in the early 1900s, the parishioners of Good Counsel outgrew the original church, which was converted into a parish school run by the Sisters of Loretto in 1908. The cornerstone of the present-day Good Counsel was laid on July 15, 1906, and the church was dedicated on Thanksgiving Day in 1907. Our Lady of Good Counsel Church is one of the best examples in all of Kansas City of Palladian architecture. The high altar of Carrara marble was donated by Mr. and Mrs. Hugh Matthews and is estimated to have cost $10,500.

SS. Peter and Paul Parish, 1929. SS. Peter and Paul Parish was founded in 1866 to serve the large German-speaking population flourishing in the city. In fact, its initial name was Immaculate Conception German Parish, perhaps because the German congregation met for Mass at the Cathedral of the Immaculate Conception. Even before the parish was established, Father Donnelly secured the assistance of Fr. Francis Ruesse in hearing confessions and providing missions to the German-speaking residents. The first canonical pastor was Fr. Herman Grosse, who arrived in 1867.

Interior of SS. Peter and Paul, 1929. Construction began in the late spring of 1868 and was completed in 1870. The church was designed by Fr. Ernest Zechenter, who stayed as the parish's pastor for 51 years. SS. Peter and Paul had the distinction of being not only the first church in Kansas City to have a pipe organ but also the first in the city to be insured against tornadoes. In 1881, Father Zechenter asked a member of the congregation who was an insurance salesman for a donation; he said he could not afford a donation, but offered three years of free tornado insurance. It was fortuitous, as the parish was struck twice by tornadoes between 1881 and 1884. The last High Mass was celebrated on January 14, 1923, and the parish was permanently closed.

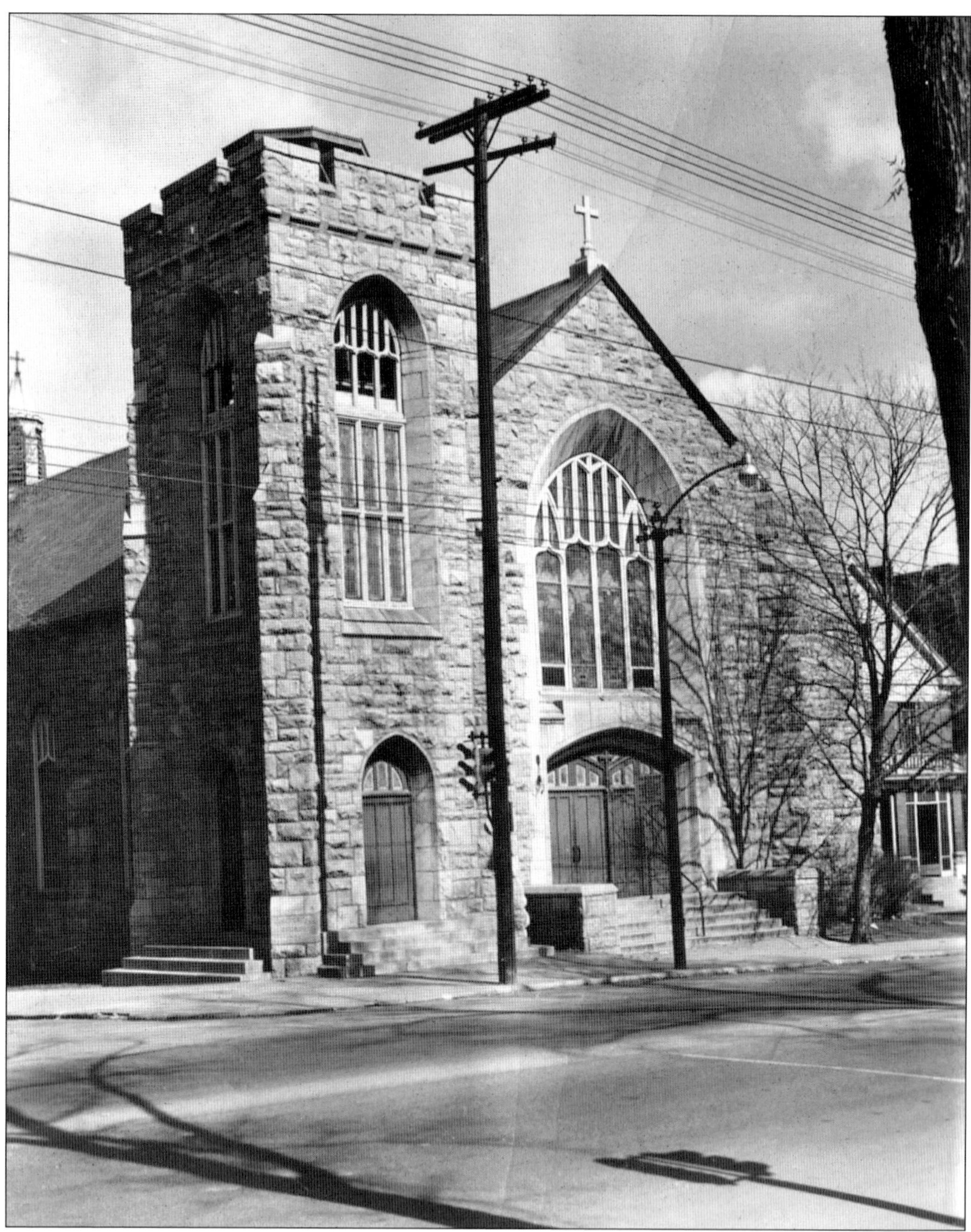

Holy Cross Parish, 1954. Holy Cross Parish was canonically established on Easter Monday in 1902. Constructed in a mostly vacant and uninhabited area between the Missouri River to the north and Independence Avenue to the south, Holy Cross began with a mere 35 Catholic families in its congregation. The parish's first pastor, Fr. John J. Hogan (not to be confused with Bishop John J. Hogan) worked with the pastor of St. Patrick Parish, Fr. Thomas Lillis (the future bishop of Kansas City), to construct the church, which first celebrated services in April 1905. By 1917, Holy Cross had grown to 350 families, showing the continued influx of Catholic immigrants into Kansas City during the 1900s.

OLD ST. PATRICK PARISH, 1904. The third parish established in Kansas City was St. Patrick in 1868. Rising out of a need to provide religious services for the overcrowded Cathedral Parish and for those who did not speak German, St. Patrick's primarily accommodated Kansas City's large number of Irish Catholics. Following the Civil War, more and more Irish migrated to Kansas City and settled principally on the east side of Downtown along Cherry, Holmes, Charlotte, and Campbell Streets. Every Catholic living east of Main Street who did not speak German belonged to the parish.

HIGH MASS AT OLD ST. PATRICK PARISH, 1959. Beginning in January 1958, the parish was officially referred to as Old St. Patrick's to differentiate it from the new St. Patrick's, which had been founded north of the Missouri River in Clay County in the former Diocese of St. Joseph. The parish is notable in the fact that during its long history, two bishops and one cardinal (Thomas Lillis, Joseph V. Sullivan, and John J. Glennon, respectively) all served as parish pastors of St. Patrick's. Today, Old St. Patrick's is one of the few parishes within the Diocese of Kansas City–St. Joseph that regularly celebrates the traditional Latin Mass.

Our Lady of Perpetual Help (Redemptorist) Parish, 1979. Though Redemptorist fathers settled in Kansas City in 1876, the current Our Lady of Perpetual Help Parish Church was not erected until 1908. At the time of construction, it was believed that Redemptorist would be the largest church west of the Mississippi River with the exception of the Mormon Temple in Salt Lake City, Utah. When the cornerstone was laid during a grand ceremony on June 21, 1908, it is believed that some 15,000 spectators were present. The parish was established within the Kerry Patch neighborhood, which was primarily an Irish enclave. But Germans, Italians, and Slovaks also attended the parish and likewise participated in the parish consecration parade. The main altar was consecrated by Bishop Thomas Lillis on June 1, 1913, although it had been provisionally installed on December 23, 1912. The altar is made of pure Italian marble and cost $10,000. In the summer of 1915, the communion rail was installed to allow five priests to simultaneously distribute communion.

Main Altar at Redemptorist Parish, 2000. The main altar of Our Lady of Perpetual Help was blessed on June 1, 1913, by Bishop Thomas Lillis of the Diocese of Kansas City. The altar was donated to the parish by the widow of Richard H. Keith and was constructed in the studios of the Deprato Statuary Company in Pietrasanta, Italy. Workmen from Italy accompanied the altar to Kansas City and oversaw its installation within the parish. It took six weeks for the altar to be completed. The primary characteristic of the altar is the Redemptorist Mother icon, which has been spread by the Redemptorist religious order since 1866. In 1879, the famous Our Lady of Perpetual Help Novena was introduced, which has since become a weekly part of thousands of Catholics' spiritual life and a central part of worship among those who attend Redemptorist parish.

JOHN J. HOGAN, BISHOP OF KANSAS CITY, 1880. By the time Bishop John J. Hogan was named to the newly created Diocese of Kansas City in 1880, the city was home to 30,000 Catholics. New challenges awaited Bishop Hogan, particularly in overseeing a diocese that comprised 23,539 square miles. The diocese's borders were vast and stretched north to the Missouri River, west to the Kansas state line, and south to the Arkansas line. Yet despite the potential pitfalls of controlling such a wide swath of territory, Hogan witnessed the Catholic population of Kansas City double to 60,000 between 1880 and 1890.

BISHOP HOGAN, C. 1900. Bishop Hogan found himself under nearly constant pressure to establish new parishes and construct schools, convents, orphanages, and other religious institutions in Kansas City. He also faced challenges in that many Catholics arriving in Kansas City did not speak English, as a continued influx of immigrants from Germany, Poland, Italy, and Sicily arrived throughout the late 19th and early 20th centuries. Like for Father Donnelly, education was central to the episcopacy of Bishop Hogan. By the time of Hogan's death in 1913, nearly 15,000 children attended Catholic schools across the city.

ICON FROM CHURCH OF OUR LADY (LEBANESE) PARISH, C. 1980. Perhaps the most intriguing parish in the history of the Diocese of Kansas City–St. Joseph was Church of Our Lady Parish. Established in the West Bottoms in 1893, the parish's Marionite congregants were from the Middle East, particularly Lebanon, and spoke mostly Arabic. The parishioners called the parish Kneest Al-Saidi, which translates into "Church of Our Lady." There was only one Mass on Sundays, and the congregation sang all the appropriate parts of the liturgy in Arabic. An instrument called an oud was used for musical accompaniment during services.

FR. JOHN YAMIN, C. 1915. Fr. John Yamin served as the only pastor of Church of Our Lady Parish from its establishment in 1893 to its closing in 1928. Born in Zakritt, near Beirut, Lebanon, in 1838, Father Yamin arrived in the United States and Kansas City in 1893 to serve the approximately 50 Syrian and Lebanese families who lived in the West Bottoms. Father Yamin was called "Hodi Hanna," which means "Father John" in the Syro-Chaldaic language. Father Yamin supplemented his income by making and selling rosaries. He never learned English and celebrated the Marionite Rite exclusively in Arabic. Upon his death in April 1928, Bishop Thomas Lillis could not find another priest who spoke Arabic or could celebrate the Marionite Rite, which forced the diocese to close the parish.

Our Lady of Sorrows Parish, c. 1940. The other principally German parish in Kansas City after SS. Peter and Paul was Our Lady of Sorrows, which was established in 1890. Bishop Hogan invited the Franciscans to establish a parish in the then-southern section of Kansas City as German Catholics began moving away from Downtown and out of the boundary of SS. Peter and Paul. The first location of Our Lady of Sorrows was on the southwest corner of Twenty-Third Street and Baltimore Avenue. However, as Kansas City expanded, the city witnessed a movement to build a new Union Station to accommodate its growing population. The Kansas City Terminal Railway purchased the land Our Lady of Sorrows occupied in 1906 for $51,000. It is believed that the general ticket office in Union Station now covers the site of the former church. The parish moved to its present site at Twenty-Sixth Street and Gillham Road.

Interior of Our Lady of Sorrows Parish, 1962. On March 25, 1922, ground breaking occurred for the present church building of Our Lady of Sorrows. The cornerstone was laid on July 30, 1922, and the first services were held on Easter of 1923. The church could hold 600 parishioners. Besides the beauty of the exterior is the distinctive altar with its large crown. Although an Episcopalian, the founder of Hallmark Cards, Joyce "J.C." Hall, would regularly pray in Our Lady of Sorrows, as the headquarters of Hallmark are near the parish. It is believed that Hall admired the altar's crown so much that it became the inspiration for the crown logo used by Hallmark.

Golden Jubilee Mass at Holy Name Parish, 1936. Formally established by Bishop Hogan in 1886, Holy Name Parish received its name because it was founded on the feast day of the Circumcision of Our Lord. This feast day celebrates the time in Jewish law when children received their names. In 1907, property on the southeast corner of Twenty-Third Street and Benton Boulevard was purchased as the final location of the parish after having previously been at Twenty-Fourth Street and College Avenue. The church was French Gothic in design and could seat 1,000 parishioners. In 1974, the parish council of Holy Name began discussions with St. Vincent and Annunciation Parishes about consolidating. On July 1, 1975, Holy Name merged with St. Vincent's and Annunciation to form Church of the Risen Christ Parish.

Sacred Heart Parish, c. 1920. Sacred Heart Parish was canonically established on April 20, 1887, with Fr. Michael J. O'Dwyer serving as the first pastor. A mostly Irish parish, Sacred Heart's parishioners celebrated their first Mass in the home of Edward Doherty, with the Doherty family's piano serving as the altar. The parish church was constructed at Twenty-Fifth Street and Madison Avenue. The bricks used in the building were from a kiln built and operated by Father O'Dwyer, and it is reported that he worked alongside the laborers and carpenters during construction.

Interior of Sacred Heart Parish, c. 1920. Sacred Heart Parish was supposedly modeled on the stone churches in western Ireland. A large Celtic cross was placed on the church tower. Sacred Heart's Irish parishioners gradually declined over the decades, and in 1990, it was announced that Sacred Heart would consolidate with Our Lady of Guadalupe Parish in order to better serve Hispanic Catholics in the neighborhood.

Bishop Thomas F. Lillis with Kansas City Priests, 1914. Ordained on August 15, 1885, Lexington, Missouri, native Bishop Thomas F. Lillis was originally the bishop of Leavenworth beginning in 1904. Prior to his elevation to the episcopacy, Lillis served as one of the original priests in the Diocese of Kansas City. He served as the first pastor of the Westport Church (Our Lady of Good Counsel) and then as the parochial administrator of St. Patrick Parish for 17 years. Lillis's episcopacy, from 1913 to 1938, was the golden age of Kansas City Catholicism.

Bishop Lillis, c. 1920. With the death of Bishop John J. Hogan in 1913, Bishop Lillis immediately set to work. Lillis saw an immense need to not only open up more effective communication with his priests across Kansas City and the diocese at large but also to reform worship practices, particularly within church music. Lillis began to regularly communicate with clergy across the city and was well-informed about parish business. Decisions that were made independently of the bishop's office were now made by the chancery administration or directly by Bishop Lillis himself. Lillis also divided the diocese into four deaneries for more efficient administration. Thirty-five parishes were opened during his tenure as bishop, and 50,000 new Catholics were welcomed into the church. Active in civic as well as religious activities, Bishop Lillis said Mass in his residence for the army heads of three European nations (French marshal Ferdinand Foch, Italian general Armando Diaz, and Belgian general Baron Alphonse Jacques de Dixmude) following the dedication of Liberty Memorial in Kansas City in 1921. Bishop Lillis died of a heart attack on December 29, 1938.

Holy Rosary Parish, c. 1950. When Italian and Sicilian immigrants arrived in Kansas City in the late 19th century, they initially had to attend the primarily Irish St. Patrick's at Eighth and Cherry Streets. As more Italian-speaking people arrived, there arose a desire to have a priest and parish of their own, as it was important to have someone who could preach and counsel congregants in their native language. In 1891, Holy Rosary Parish was formally established. By 1929, Holy Rosary was primarily a Sicilian parish: 85 percent of members were of Sicilian heritage, with 10 percent coming from southern Italy and only 5 percent from northern Italy.

Golden Jubilee of Holy Rosary Parish, 1942. The newly founded Scalabrini Fathers were willing to send a priest to Kansas City, and in October 1890, Fr. Ferdinando Santipolo, PSSC, arrived. The Scalabrini Fathers were especially important in the success of Italian Catholicism in the area. Holy Rosary Parish was in most regards the church of the poor in the North End, but due to the hard work of Father Santipolo and the Scalabrini Fathers, Holy Rosary became increasingly successful throughout the 20th century.

Blessed Sacrament Parish. Founded in 1909, Blessed Sacrament Parish was created out of need to provide services for Catholics who lived south of Annunciation Parish and east of St. James Parish. The Blessed Sacrament church building was considered by many to be a work of art. It was constructed of Bedford stone and was the first cut-stone church in Kansas City. The interior was stenciled throughout by local artist Dante Cosentino, who was noted for his exquisite work in Catholic churches across Kansas City. The Architectural League of Kansas City gave Blessed Sacrament an honorable mention for Outstanding Building in Effective Design in 1927. Blessed Sacrament closed in 1991 and was absorbed by Church of the Risen Christ Parish.

OUR LADY OF GUADALUPE PARISH, 2001. Despite a presence in the area dating to the Santa Fe Trail, Mexican Americans began to increasingly reside along Southwest Boulevard beginning around 1910. Those of Mexican heritage arrived in Kansas City primarily for two reasons: opportunities for work during World War I and displacement by the Mexican Revolution. In the spring of 1914, the parish of Our Lady of Guadalupe was established to serve the Mexican community in the city.

ANNUNCIATION BALDACHINO AND ALTAR, 2000. Annunciation Parish was one of three parishes created out of the original St. John Francis Regis (the future Cathedral of the Immaculate Conception) Parish. Canonically established on May 25, 1872, Annunciation was in one of the more raucous neighborhoods of Kansas City, which was filled with saloons, gambling, and vice of all kinds. An original church was erected in 1872, but the parish undertook an extravagant campaign to build a new church beginning in 1920. The new church was completed and dedicated in May 1924. The unique and indeed astonishing feature of the new church was the baldachino and altar. The baldachino, 34 feet tall and composed of Italian marble, was designed by Deprato Service in Chicago. The marble altar, itself ornate in design and extravagant in price, costing $1,500, was given to the parish in 1903 by a prominent parishioner and devout Catholic, James "Big Jim" Pendergast, the brother of the infamous Kansas City boss Tom Pendergast. Pendergast donated the altar in memory of his deceased wife.

St. Stanislaus Parish. St. Stanislaus Parish was founded in 1913 by Polish immigrants who arrived in Kansas City between 1910 and 1912. Most of the men were employed by the American Radiator Company in Buffalo, New York, and relocated when the company moved its headquarters to Kansas City. They settled by and large in a neighborhood called Centropolis. Polish ethnic life at St. Stanislaus was vibrant, with the St. Stanislaus Society organized in 1912 along with the Polish Roman Catholic Union Zjednoczenie, Lodge No. 788.

Visitation of the Blessed Mother Parish. The founding of Visitation of the Blessed Mother Parish in 1909 emerged from a desire for Catholicism to expand into the south side of Kansas City. The current church was dedicated in 1917 and was built in the Spanish style. It is thought that it was modeled after either the Santa Barbara or San Gabriel Mission. What is certain is that the Spanish vernacular architecture was attractive to Kansas City real estate developer J.C. Nichols. When he was developing his new business and apartment district near Forty-Seventh Street, Nichols used photographs of Visitation in his company's advertising folders. Nichols's development utilized Spanish architecture throughout and became the Country Club Plaza.

Interior of Visitation Parish. In 1937, the interior of Visitation Parish underwent a massive renovation. The studio of James B. Gantt in Kansas City, Kansas, oversaw the design. The redesign called for a 16-panel mural portraying the mysteries of the rosary. The original communion rail remained, as it was a gift to the parish from "Boss Tom" Pendergast and his wife in memory of James "Big Jim" Pendergast. Once again in 1974, Visitation underwent extensive renovation, but this time the only parts of the original church that were left were the building itself and the bell tower.

VESPERS BEFORE INSTALLATION OF BISHOP EDWIN V. O'HARA, 1939. Upon the death of Bishop Thomas Lillis in 1938, Bishop Edwin V. O'Hara of the Diocese of Great Falls, Montana, was named the third bishop of the Diocese of Kansas City. Before arriving in Kansas City, Bishop O'Hara garnered a reputation as a forward-thinking leader in Catholic education, liturgical renewal, and more involvement of the laity in church affairs. O'Hara is credited with beginning the first weekly newspaper in the diocese's history with the establishment of the *Catholic Register* and later the *Catholic Reporter*. He participated in the rejuvenation of the Confraternity of Christian Doctrine, an organization providing religious education for Catholic children attending public schools.

ARCHBISHOP EDWIN V. O'HARA. Catholic education in general became a hallmark of O'Hara's episcopacy in Kansas City, as he consistently worked to expand high schools owned and operated by the diocese. By 1940, the first three high schools supported by the diocese (Cardinal Glennon, Bishop Lillis, and Bishop Hogan) opened in Kansas City to provide a quality Catholic education for every child in the city. O'Hara was appointed archbishop ad personam in June 1954 and died on September 11, 1956, in Milan, Italy. He is buried at Mount Olivet Cemetery in Kansas City.

Assumption Parish. The establishment of Assumption Parish occurred with only 68 people in a rented building at 3423 Garner Street. The parish received its name because the first Mass was held on the Feast of the Assumption, August 15, 1909. The first church building was constructed in 1910 at Thirty-Second and Lexington Streets, and congregants attended Mass there until 1921, when the parish moved to 318 Benton Boulevard. The cornerstone for the new church was laid on October 13, 1922, with 3,000 people in attendance. Chester Dean of White and Dean Architecture constructed the new church using a combination of Romanesque and mission architectural designs. Dante Cosentino adorned the interior with white and gold trim depicting angels. He also painted a dove of peace holding a strand of wheat in its beak above the altar. At the time, Assumption was considered one of the finest pieces of architecture in Kansas City.

Assumption Parishioners Leaving Mass, 1960. Assumption underwent a major renovation project in 1967. The entire church was repainted, and the sanctuary was entirely renovated. In 1990, it was announced by the Diocesan Planning Effort that Assumption Parish would merge with St. Francis Seraph and St. John the Baptist Parishes. The consolidation became official on February 4, 1991, and the amalgamated parish was renamed St. Anthony of Padua.

IMMACULATE HEART OF MARY PARISH, 1945. Established in 1937, St. Mary Parish was officially renamed Immaculate Heart of Mary Parish in 1959. It was formed out of the boundaries of St. Therese Little Flower, Blessed Sacrament, St. James, St. Louis, and St. Francis Xavier Parishes. Although beginning with only 170 families, the parish consisted of 450 families by the 1950s. The church was designed by Samuel W. Bihr in a mission style. The altar for Immaculate Heart of Mary came from the old Annunciation Parish. In an effort to raise morale within the parish during World War II, through the efforts of Bishop Edwin V. O'Hara, the War Production Board granted the parish permission to construct a new chapel east of the original church. The new chapel was dedicated on August 5, 1945. It was decreed by the Diocese of Kansas City–St. Joseph on July 1, 1969, that the parish would be suppressed, and its territory was assumed by St. Louis Parish.

Msgr. Peter Kennedy in Back of St. Elizabeth Church, c. 1960. The first parish created under the episcopacy of Bishop Thomas F. Lillis was St. Elizabeth in 1917. The parish was named for its copatronage of Saint Elizabeth of Hungary and Saint Elizabeth Ann Seton, the first American-born saint. The parish at first met in a rented storefront on Seventy-Fifth Street and began with around 150 people. Land was purchased in late 1919 for a church to be constructed on a square block between Main and Baltimore Streets and Seventy-Fourth Street Terrace and Seventy-Fifth Street. The church was completed in the fall of 1922 and could seat 460 worshippers. The parish community grew steadily between 1922 and the early 1950s and was enough to warrant the building of a new church. Ground was broken in 1960, and the new church was dedicated on September 21, 1961.

St. John the Baptist Parish, 1957. St. John the Baptist Parish was created on the boundary of St. Patrick Parish and was officially established by Bishop John J. Hogan in February 1882. Although initially an Irish parish, over time, St. John the Baptist's community came to be comprised of a majority of Catholics with Italian and Sicilian heritage. Indeed, by 1950, the parish was over 90 percent Italian and Sicilian.

Interior of St. John the Baptist Parish, 1957. By the 1960s, much of Kansas City north of Independence Avenue was undergoing urban renewal. Many of the old Italian and Sicilian families began moving out of northeast Kansas City, particularly after 1963–1964, when the Osteopathic Hospital and College purchased the homes of approximately 200 parishioners. On October 12, 1990, the diocese announced the parish would consolidate with Assumption and St. Francis Seraph Parishes and be renamed St. Anthony of Padua in 1991.

St. Aloysius Parish. The creation of St. Aloysius Parish can be traced to 1885, when the Jesuits pursued a site to establish a church and school in Kansas City. Bishop Hogan agreed to allow the Jesuits to visit Kansas City, and upon their arrival, at the recommendation of Bishop Hogan, a site was chosen to build their parish at the corner of Eleventh and Prospect Streets. Masses began to be celebrated in January 1886. The cornerstone was laid on July 27, 1890, by Bishop Hogan and Fr. Henry J. Votel, SJ. Mass was first celebrated in the new church on February 22, 1891. The Benedictines took over St. Aloysius from the Jesuits in July 1959. The church was demolished in 1970, with every brick salvaged and all statues and the altar saved for the construction of the new church, which was completed in March 1970.

St. Louis, King of France Parish. St. Louis Parish was established on July 1, 1919, by decree of Bishop Thomas F. Lillis. Bishop Lillis assigned L. Curtis Tiernan as the parish's first pastor, which he readily accepted. Father Tiernan had recently been released from active duty in the US Army after serving in France during World War I. There is no other information as to how the name for the parish was chosen, but it was understood that Bishop Lillis wished to expand the church into the Swope Park district. Father Tiernan's mother furnished the candlesticks for the parish, while all the other fixtures were borrowed from Blessed Sacrament Parish. The parish first gathered in rented space at Flacy's Hall at Fifty-Sixth Street and Swope Parkway. Ground was broken for the church on October 16, 1919, and construction was completed on May 23, 1920. The first Mass was celebrated in St. Louis Parish on the same day.

St. Stephen Parish. In 1888, in an effort to expand the church into the Sheffield district, Bishop John J. Hogan purchased land between Bennington and Newton Avenues overlooking the Missouri River and Washington Park. There was a need for a new parish to provide worship for a large number of recently arrived German and Irish Catholic workers due to the relocation of two companies into Kansas City—the Kansas City Switch and Frog Company and the Pennsylvania Car Works. The cornerstone for what became St. Stephen Parish was laid in 1888, and Mass began being celebrated in 1889. Construction for a new church began in 1916, and the St. Stephen's community celebrated Mass in its new home on Christmas morning in 1921. The new church cost $50,000 to build. In 1985, the Kansas City Landmarks Commission designated St. Stephen's a historic landmark. Due to declining attendance by the late 1980s and early 1990s, the diocese recommended that four parishes (St. Stephen, St. Michael, St. Stanislaus, and Holy Trinity) amalgamate into one parish to be located at St. Stephen's. On February 4, 1991, the parish was renamed Our Lady of Peace.

Msgr. L. Curtis Tiernan (far right) with Harry S. Truman, 1954. One of the more well-known and influential priests of the Diocese of Kansas City–St. Joseph was Msgr. Louis Curtis Tiernan. Born in St. Louis, Tiernan moved to Kansas City at a young age with his family. He graduated from the Pontifical North American College in Rome and was ordained to the priesthood in 1910. Tiernan was approached by a group of young Irish Catholic Kansas Citians wishing to obtain him as their chaplain when the United States entered World War I in 1917. Enlisting in the Army in what became Battery D of the 129th Field Artillery, Tiernan became regimental chaplain and developed a close relationship with the battery's commander, Harry S. Truman. After World War I, Tiernan returned to Kansas City and became the first pastor of St. Louis Parish and later was the rector of St. Patrick's. Returning to the service in 1928, Tiernan became the head of all chaplains of the European theater in World War II, a position on the staff of Gen. Dwight D. Eisenhower.

First Renovation of the Cathedral, 1955. Bishop Edwin V. O'Hara made the decision for the cathedral to undergo a massive renovation in preparation for the parish's diamond jubilee in 1955. When Bishop O'Hara requested an investigation into the planned renovation, it was discovered by the diocesan contractors that the supports and wooden beams that were part of the cathedral's original construction in 1882 had dry-rotted. The artist chosen to lead the design of the cathedral renovation was Charlton Fortune.

Cathedral with New Altar Mosaic, 1955. Charlton Fortune was known for her impressionist pieces and innovative ecclesiastical designs. O'Hara first invited Fortune to Kansas City in the 1940s, and her work was extensive throughout the city in parishes such as St. Peter, Christ the King, and St. Francis Xavier. Fortune's divisive element of the renovation project was the large mosaic of the Blessed Mother above the altar. Fortune did not want the mosaic to draw attention away from the altar of the church, and gave it a shadowy appearance. Generally, the mosaic was not well received by parishioners and many others in Kansas City.

Golden Dome of Cathedral, 1961. Part of the skyline of downtown Kansas City is the iconic dome of the Cathedral of the Immaculate Conception. However, the dome, as well as the cupola and cross, were not gilded until 1960. The original structure was made of copper, but by 1959, it had begun to deteriorate due to the elements. The diocese contracted Herman Sager and a crew of three steeplejacks from St. Louis to apply gold leaf to the dome. All the oxidized copper was removed, along with approximately a ton and a half of rusted iron railing from the cupola. After extensive cleaning and the application of zinc bromide, 222 rolls of gold leaf were applied. The project was an immense undertaking, as the cross itself stands 13 feet tall with arms 8 feet wide. Adding in the cross, the structure stands 185 feet off the ground. In total, the project cost $20,366.71.

Mass at St. Francis Xavier Parish, 1959. In early 1909, Bishop Hogan was asked to establish a Jesuit college that would lie within the boundary of a Jesuit parish. On July 1, 1909, the diocese established St. Francis Xavier Parish at Fifty-Second Street and Troost Avenue. The first church was constructed in 1910, but the existing church was built beginning in 1948. The cornerstone was laid on June 26, 1949, and the church was blessed on July 4, 1950. At the time, St. Francis Xavier was alleged to be the most modern Catholic church in the Midwest. A fascinating design aspect of the parish is that St. Francis Xavier is built in the form of a fish, an ancient Christian symbol for Jesus Christ.

Installation of Bishop Charles H. Helmsing, 1962. Serving first as bishop of the newly created Diocese of Springfield–Cape Girardeau from 1956 until his assignment as bishop of the Diocese of Kansas City–St. Joseph in 1962, Bishop Charles Herman Helmsing was a key figure not only in the Second Vatican Council but also in a movement of Christian unity across denominations within Kansas City and across the diocese.

Bishop Helmsing at Second Vatican Council, 1962. In 1965, Bishop Helmsing was made a member of the US Bishops' Commission on ecumenical affairs, and in turn became chairman of the subcommittee for discussions between the Catholic and Episcopal Churches on denominational cooperation. One of three Americans named as Pope Paul VI's secretariat for promoting Christian unity, Bishop Helmsing was instrumental in the cooperation among Kansas City Christians for the implementation of Vatican II changes after 1962 and wider collaboration with non-Catholics in the area.

GROUND BREAKING FOR ST. ANDREW THE APOSTLE PARISH, 1965. Canonically established on July 1, 1964, the original name for St. Andrew the Apostle Parish was Mary, Queen of the Universe Parish. The first congregants attended Mass in the Mellody-McGilley-Eylar Funeral Home chapel on Vivion Road. The church was built on land purchased from John and Mary Johnson, and its boundaries were carved out of other Northland parishes of St. Charles Borromeo and St. James in Liberty.

DEDICATION OF ST. ANDREW THE APOSTLE PARISH, 1966. The parish broke ground for its new church building on April 24, 1965, with the first Mass celebrated there on February 20, 1966. Herman A. Scharhag was hired to design the church, and the total cost of the building was $73,000. The first pews were given to St. Andrew's by St. Catherine of Siena Parish in South Kansas City. St. Andrew the Apostle Parish seats approximately 125 people.

St. Bernadette Parish. The diocese determined in 1958 that a new parish should be formed to the northwest of Raytown but to the south of Leeds. The new parish would seat roughly 600 people and would be built somewhere in the vicinity of Sni-A-Bar Road and Blue Ridge Cutoff. When the congregation of this new parish met for the first time in June 1958, a name had not yet been chosen. The first pastor, Fr. John R. Quinn, noted in his homily on June 15, 1958, that the Blessed Virgin appeared to Saint Bernadette and that the new parish community should pray to her in helping the parish begin. Accordingly, from that time on, the parish was called St. Bernadette. The mayors of both Kansas City and Raytown attended the ground-breaking ceremony for St. Bernadette Parish Church on February 7, 1960. The architectural firm chosen to construct St. Bernadette's was Shaughnessey, Bower, and Grimaldi, with J.E. Dunn Construction Company serving as general contractor.

St. Catherine of Siena Parish. Although Bishop Lillis was convinced to establish a parish in Hickman Mills in South Kansas City, the preliminary outlook seemed rather bleak. When St. Catherine of Siena was founded in 1925, only 35 Catholics could be found living in the area. The original parishioners of St. Catherine's gathered in the home of Frank and Catherine Walsh for the first Mass on November 22, 1925. Bishop Lillis gave the parish its name due to his fondness for the parish's benefactor, Catherine Walsh. In 1926, a church was built on land that had been donated to the diocese by the Walsh family between 105th and 106th Streets facing Grandview Road. The first Mass celebrated in the church itself took place on Christmas Day in 1926. A new brick church was built in 1956, and the parish community worshipped in that space until the current church was constructed in December 1974.

ST. CHARLES BORROMEO PARISH, 1964. The first Mass for St. Charles Borromeo Parish was said on Easter Sunday in April 1947. Though in Kansas City, because the parish was located in Clay County, St. Charles Borromeo Parish was under the jurisdiction of the Diocese of St. Joseph until 1956, when the Dioceses of Kansas City and St. Joseph merged. At the time, the parish contained close to 85 families. The original parish church was actually a surplus Quonset hut that was used as an Army chapel during World War II. The chapel was purchased in Coffeyville, Kansas; disassembled by parishioners who traveled to Kansas to pick it up; and then transported back to Kansas City, where it was reassembled. The parish was named in honor of the bishop of St. Joseph, Charles LeBlond. The current church building was constructed in 1955 and dedicated on September 3, 1956.

Our Lady of Lourdes Parish, Raytown. By 1946, Bishop Edwin V. O'Hara and his chancellor, Msgr. George King, often visited the recently developed Mount Olivet Cemetery on Blue Ridge Boulevard. Both clergymen frequently discussed why there was not a parish in Raytown close to the cemetery. A caretaker of Mount Olivet, Marcus Lampton, formally requested that a parish be established in the Laurel Heights neighborhood, and Bishop O'Hara stated that if Lampton could get enough signatures, a parish would be created. Lampton managed to obtain the signatures of 50 families, and Bishop O'Hara agreed to found what became Our Lady of Lourdes Parish.

Catechetical Sunday at Our Lady of Lourdes, 1985. The ground breaking for Our Lady of Lourdes Parish took place on July 4, 1948. Like St. Charles Borromeo, the first parish church was an Army chapel; this one had been used at Camp Crowder in southwestern Missouri. The Army chapel was used as a place of worship until the current Our Lady of Lourdes Church was dedicated on October 23, 1949.

St. Patrick North Parish, 1970. Prior to the establishment of St. Patrick North Parish in 1924, Catholics who lived in Kansas City north of the Missouri River had limited options for worship. Their choices were to go south of the river and attend St. Patrick Parish or travel to Liberty or Platte City. More often than not, families chose to have Mass celebrated in their own residences, primarily by Fr. Edward Mallen, the pastor at Liberty.

Golden Jubilee Mass at St. Patrick North Parish, 1974. Parishioners of St. Patrick North began attending services between a hut owned by the Knights of Columbus in North Kansas City and Deister's Settlement in Platte County. In 1961, ground was broken for the current church for St. Patrick North at Forty-Second Terrace in the Northland of Kansas City; it was dedicated the same year.

St. Augustine Parish, 1966. Following the conclusion of World War I, Kansas City began to expand southward. Bishop Thomas F. Lillis sought to found new parishes in South Kansas City once the city limits were extended to Seventy-Ninth Street. Wishing to seize upon the large number of Catholics living in the Marlborough district, Bishop Lillis purchased the abandoned Marlborough Presbyterian Church at Seventy-Ninth Street and Paseo.

Kansas City Philharmonic Playing at St. Augustine Parish, 1978. The new parish was dedicated as St. Augustine's to honor the patron saint of the first pastor, Fr. August J. Koehler. The first Mass was celebrated on November 4, 1923. The diocese announced that it would close the parish on October 12, 1990. In February 1991, St. Augustine Parish was renamed Church of the Holy Martyrs by the Vietnamese Catholic community that relocated from northeast Kansas City.

St. Therese North Parish, c. 1975. St. Therese North Parish was established on Easter Sunday, April 9, 1950. The first Mass was celebrated in the funeral home chapel belonging to Leland Francis. In October 1950, land was purchased for the present site of the parish on Highway 9 in Kansas City North. The ground breaking occurred on the Feast of Our Lady of Lourdes, June 10, 1951, with Bishop Charles LeBlond of the Diocese of St. Joseph officiating. St. Therese Parish School was opened in September 1951, and a convent was built for the Sisters of Charity of Leavenworth in 1955. The Sisters of Charity and later the Sisters of St. Francis in Savannah occupied the convent until 1984, when it was repurposed as office space for the parish staff.

Bishop John J. Sullivan, 1977. On August 17, 1977, Charles H. Helmsing retired as the bishop of Kansas City–St. Joseph. His successor was the bishop of Grand Island, Nebraska, John J. Sullivan. Bishop Sullivan was already incredibly active, having served on numerous committees with the US Conference of Catholic Bishops. Sullivan's energy once he became the ordinary of the Diocese of Kansas City–St. Joseph was focused on parish-based renewal initiatives, which included an increased number of the laity involved in ministry. Bishop Sullivan also turned his attention toward assisting the poor as well as alleviating the plight of racial minorities and increasing their educational opportunities in inner-city Kansas City. Considered a masterful storyteller and humorous, Sullivan resigned as bishop of Kansas City–St. Joseph on June 22, 1993, after being diagnosed with Parkinson's. He died on February 11, 2001.

CHURCH OF THE HOLY MARTYRS, C. 1991. The Church of the Holy Martyrs was formally established on February 17, 1991. The predominantly Vietnamese parish was named for the 117 Vietnamese martyrs who were canonized by Pope John Paul II on June 19, 1988, at St. Peter's Basilica in Rome. The parish was founded as a "personal" parish, meaning that there was no parish boundary, and anyone of Vietnamese origin could join.

INTERIOR OF THE CHURCH OF THE HOLY MARTYRS, C. 1991. After South Vietnam fell in 1975, Vietnamese Catholics immigrated to the United States and settled in the Columbus Park area of Kansas City. In 1976, the Vietnamese Mutual Association was formed with a number of goals, including the preservation of Catholic identity for the refugees. Being situated near Columbus Park, Holy Rosary Parish was designated as the site for religious services conducted in Vietnamese. In 1990, the Vietnamese Catholic Community relocated to the former St. Augustine's Church at Seventy-Ninth Street and Paseo.

Community One Mass at Trolley Barn, 1968. The experimental Catholic community known as Community One was formed in late 1967. The idea behind the community was the celebration of a more personal and expressive liturgy. In March 1968, Community One met at the Trolley Barn in Kansas City for Mass and events.

Mass at Trolley Barn for Community One, 1968. Community One was not the only name proposed. Community of Resurrection, Shalom, Community of Life, and Community of Pope John XXIII were just some of the names put forth. It shortly became evident that the space at the Trolley Barn was too small for Mass or religious education for children. Community One moved to Bishop Hogan High School and then to Notre Dame de Scion at Thirty-Seventh and Locust Streets. Community One dissolved in the 1970s.

LITURGICAL DANCE PRODUCTION OF *PSALTERION* AT CHURCH OF THE RISEN CHRIST, 1978. The Church of the Risen Christ was officially formed on July 1, 1975, through the merging of St. Vincent, Holy Name, and Annunciation Parishes. Annunciation Parish was chosen to be the site for the establishment of Risen Christ. Though "Church of the Risen Christ" was chosen by the community, Church of the Resurrection, St. Charles Lwanga and Companions, and Mary, Holy Mother of God were other names that were proposed. Many parishioners of Risen Christ were members of the black Catholic community in Kansas City. Beginning in 1977, liturgical dance celebrations began not only for the traditional Stations of the Cross but also for other parts of Catholic liturgy. These dramas involved dance, monologues, and music in celebration of Mass.

Dedication of Holy Family Parish, 1982. Catholics worshipped in what is now referred to as Kansas City North, between Liberty and Nashua, as far back as 1912 though not in an organized parish community until the 1980s. Fr. Edward Mallen, the priest of St. James Parish in Liberty during the 1910s, ministered to Catholics who traveled to Nashua and Liberty for Mass at that time. By 1979, it became clear that a viable parish could be created in Kansas City North. The territory for the nascent community was taken from the boundaries of St. Charles Borromeo and founded along Ninety-Sixth Street in the Northland. Ten acres were purchased from Hugh J. Zimmer for $100,000 in 1980 for the site of the parish church. The name chosen for the new community was Holy Family, as the Vatican declared the 1980s the "Decade of the Family."

DIOCESAN PILGRIMAGE TO SEE POPE JOHN PAUL II, 1979. The Blessed Virgin Mary had been declared by the bishops of the Catholic Church in the United States as the nation's patroness in 1846. That same year, the Lowell, Massachusetts, *Courier Journal* wrote that a national Marian shrine was to be built in Washington, DC. The Diocese of Kansas City–St. Joseph organized a diocesan pilgrimage to visit the Basilica of the National Shrine of the Immaculate Conception. Parishioners from Our Lady of Perpetual Help (Redemptorist) Parish, along with other parishes from the diocese, traveled to Washington, DC, in 1979 to honor the 125th anniversary of the declaration of the Immaculate Conception as the national shrine. Redemptorist parishioners carried a banner they hoped the Polish Pope John Paul II would see. The banner reads "Long Live the Holy Father."

Bishop John J. Sullivan Cutting Ribbon for Dedication of Holy Family Parish, 1982. Holy Family's church design was impacted heavily by the concept of family and the importance of the closeness of the parish community with one another. The layout of the church and the architectural motif strongly resemble a private home. The design and construction of Holy Family became very much an extensive affair, with many people involved in the process. Fr. Patrick Rush, the newly assigned parish pastor in the fall of 1980, contacted the College of Architecture and Design at Kansas State University in Manhattan to see if any architectural students were interested in doing initial designs for the church. Seventy-five students proposed designs, with the parish community deciding the best plan for the church. Ground was broken in August 1981, and the parish was dedicated in 1982.

Bishop Raymond J. Boland, 1993. Following the retirement of Bishop John J. Sullivan on June 22, 1993, after being diagnosed with Parkinson's, the Vatican chose as his replacement the gregarious, Irish-born bishop of Birmingham, Alabama, Raymond James Boland. Attending seminary at All Hallows College in Dublin, Boland was ordained in 1957 for the Archdiocese of Washington, DC. He was appointed bishop of Birmingham in 1988 and was installed as bishop of Kansas City–St. Joseph in 1993.

Bishop Boland, 1993. Boland began his tenure as the fourth bishop of Kansas City–St. Joseph in a tumultuous secular and religious era in Kansas City's history. Kansas City was in the beginning stages of recovery from the disastrous flood of 1993. Simultaneously, the Catholic population was leaving the inner city, and the number of those entering the priesthood was dwindling. Warm-hearted yet decisive as the diocese's ordinary, Bishop Boland was instantly beloved by Catholics in Kansas City when he earmarked $12,000 out of the $15,000 arranged for his installation reception to go to flood victims.

St. Anthony Parish, 1991. As membership steadily declined during the 1970s and 1980s in parishes in northeast Kansas City, the Diocese of Kansas City–St. Joseph determined that the parishes of Assumption, St. Francis Seraph, and St. John the Baptist would be consolidated into a single parish to be located at Assumption Parish. The amalgamation of these three parishes was decreed by the diocese on October 12, 1993.

Palm Sunday Mass at St. Anthony Parish, c. 1990s. The parishioners from the three merged parishes all voted on names put forth for the new parish community. By popular demand, St. Anthony of Padua was chosen and was announced by the diocese on January 13, 1991. The name became official on February 4, 1991. The first Masses were celebrated at St. Anthony on February 9, 1991.

SECOND CATHEDRAL RENOVATION, 2003. Wishing to return the ornate design of the Cathedral of the Immaculate Conception, Bishop Boland assembled a panel of architects led by cathedral rector and Second Vatican Council expert Msgr. Ernest J. Fiedler to explore the estimated cost of renovation. Boland announced that the goal was $25 million to not only fund the renovation project but also update local Catholic high schools and augment the priests' retirement fund. Ultimately, the campaign met its desired goal; the cathedral's renovation began in 2001 and was completed in 2003, with the cathedral being rededicated on February 22, 2003. A unique aspect of the second renovation project was that lay people across the diocese were asked to provide input on how the cathedral's new interior should look. Boland encouraged Kansas City Catholics to participate directly in design plans and attend a series of meetings hosted at the cathedral along with both clergy and lay leaders.

Three

Catholic Education in Kansas City

When the education-minded Jesuits returned to Kansas City in 1886 to found St. Aloysius Parish, they immediately turned their attention to the creation of a Catholic college for young men. Through persistency and hard work, the Jesuits finally established Rockhurst College in 1910. The founding of the College of St. Teresa—later to be renamed Avila College—followed in 1916. However, the goal for Catholic education across Kansas City was rooted not in providing Catholic post-secondary educational institutions but Catholic education for all. The episcopacy of Bishop Edwin V. O'Hara served as the benchmark for the spreading of Catholic education not just to the college-aged young but to children as well.

O'Hara's first homily as bishop of Kansas City in 1939 further reinforced the prelate's passion for education for the young. "And if there be one work more than another which I shall commend to your devoted care," Bishop O'Hara noted to his listeners, "it will be the one signified by my Episcopal motto: 'Permit the little children to come unto me and forbid them not.' I charge you today as your Bishop with the responsibility for the religious and moral training of all the Youth of this great Diocese. The future is with the youth of today." With those words, Bishop O'Hara laid the groundwork for the eventual founding of Catholic secondary educational institutions and parish schools within Kansas City.

Blessed Sacrament Parish School Class Photograph, c. 1920s. Blessed Sacrament Parish School opened on September 11, 1916. The school began with only 13 students across four grades. Enrollment steadily rose, with 150 pupils enrolled by 1920. The Sisters of Charity of Leavenworth operated the school between 1916 and 1982. The school was originally located in three classrooms above the church, but in 1941, a standalone building for the school was blessed by Bishop Edwin V. O'Hara. Shaughnessy and Bower designed the building, and the school's architecture mimicked the Romanesque style of the parish church. The new school could accommodate 400 students. In 1955, a library and two additional classrooms were added. St. Louis Parish School and Blessed Sacrament Parish School consolidated in 1974, with the children who attended Blessed Sacrament moving to the St. Louis facility.

Sacred Heart Parish School Baseball Team, 1929. Like the church for Sacred Heart Parish, the school was constructed in 1887 using bricks forged in the kiln of the parish pastor, Fr. Michael J. O'Dwyer. Father O'Dwyer personally worked in the brickyard making the bricks for the new school and is reported to have assisted the laborers and bricklayers in building the school itself. The Sisters of Providence of St. Mary-of-the-Woods, Indiana, instructed Sacred Heart's pupils after arriving in Kansas City in January 1889. The Sisters of Providence left Kansas City in 1894, and the Sisters of Loretto came to take their place. Originally, the parish school was Sacred Heart Academy until the construction of Loretto Academy in 1901. During the 1930s, Sacred Heart Parish School was the site of a night school that taught courses in English, cooking, and bookkeeping. By 1934, thirty-four adults were registered for the night school.

WAR SAVINGS BOND BOOTH AT ASSUMPTION SCHOOL, 1944. When the Sisters of St. Joseph of Carondelet arrived to instruct the students attending Assumption Parish School, no school building existed. Between 1913 and 1922, the first floor of the parish rectory was used for instruction. There were only two classrooms available, while a house was purchased on Benton Boulevard for the fourth- and fifth-grade students. This building was known as "Junior University." In 1922, when Assumption Parish opened its new church, a school was also built for all grades. Out of the 152 school-age children registered at the parish, 142 were enrolled in the parish school. Attendance increased enough to justify the construction of a new school, which was completed and blessed by Archbishop O'Hara in September 1954. Assumption School consolidated with other local schools in northeast Kansas City in 1970. In May 1981, Assumption School once again consolidated, this time with St. John the Baptist and Holy Rosary, forming St. John Tri-School.

NOTRE DAME DE SCION CLASS PHOTOGRAPH, 1933. The Sisters of Scion arrived in the United States in 1892 and began teaching in the Kansas City area in 1912 at Annunciation Parish School. Desiring to establish a French academy, the Sisters at first taught kindergarten-aged students at the Lockridge Home at Thirtieth and Prospect Streets. The first high school class graduated from Notre Dame de Scion in 1923.

NOTRE DAME DE SCION HIGH SCHOOL, c. 1963. Notre Dame de Scion celebrated its 50th anniversary in Kansas City by opening the current location of the high school on Wornall Road. Ground breaking took place on May 27, 1961, with construction beginning in October 1961. The school was blessed by Bishop Charles H. Helmsing on September 8, 1961. In 1985, Notre Dame de Scion was recognized by the US Department of Education as well as the National Council of Private Education as an outstanding educational institution.

GROUND BREAKING FOR CARDINAL GLENNON HIGH SCHOOL, 1940. Bishop O'Hara consistently spoke about improving the Catholic educational experience in Kansas City during his episcopacy. In particular, O'Hara felt that more Catholic high schools needed to be established and operated by the diocese itself rather than by individual religious orders. Most of all, he believed that Catholic education needed to be coeducational. In 1940, the diocese opened the doors to Cardinal Glennon High School at 134 North Hardesty Avenue as the first coed Catholic high school in Kansas City.

CARDINAL GLENNON HIGH SCHOOL, 1949. The Sisters of Mercy operated Cardinal Glennon High School. Prior to teaching at Cardinal Glennon, the Sisters taught at St. Agnes Academy, which was a girls-only institution. At the urging of Bishop O'Hara, the Sisters altered their curriculum and began accepting male pupils in the fall of 1940. Cardinal Glennon High School closed in 1971, when it merged with St. Mary High School in Independence.

Holy Cross School Seventh-Grade Picture, 1956. Holy Cross Parish School was established as a school for boys in 1902. At the time, there was no facility for male pupils, so boys were allowed to attend the all-girls St. Agnes Academy at the corner of Scarritt and Hardesty Avenues. In 1913, an addition was built onto Holy Cross church that was turned into an educational space for boys. A standalone school was built for boys in 1923. The Sisters of Mercy staffed the Holy Cross School at 5108 St. John Avenue. Male students attended school there until September 1962, when a new school was constructed at 121 North Quincy Avenue and dedicated by Bishop John Cody. In 1975, Holy Cross School expanded its curriculum, adding a kindergarten.

CORNERSTONE LAYING FOR BISHOP LILLIS HIGH SCHOOL, 1941. Named in honor of the former bishop of Kansas City, Thomas F. Lillis, Bishop Lillis High School was established on April 7, 1940, and constructed at 3740 Forest Street. It was the second coeducational Catholic high school founded by Bishop O'Hara following the establishment of Cardinal Glennon High School in 1940. The cornerstone was laid on February 22, 1941.

BLESSING LIBRARY OF BISHOP LILLIS HIGH SCHOOL, 1941. Bishop O'Hara blessed Bishop Lillis High School on April 14, 1941. At the time, Bishop Lillis High School was the largest Diocesan-operated Catholic high school. The brick building was four stories tall with 16 classrooms that had a capacity of up to 45 students per class. In 1978, the diocese recognized that attendance was declining, and the decision was made to close Bishop Lillis High in May 1979.

LORETTO ACADEMY, 1966. Loretto Academy was opened as an all-girls school in September 1901. Operated by the Sisters of Loretto, the academy began with 21 students at Thirty-Fifth Street and Broadway Boulevard. On October 20, 1902, ground was broken for a new school at Thirty-Ninth Street and Roanoke Road. The cornerstone for the new Loretto Academy was laid on April 24, 1903. The Sisters of Loretto occupied the new Loretto Academy on August 28, 1903, and classroom instruction began on September 15, 1903.

CLASSROOM IN LORETTO ACADEMY, 1966. Providing enough space to house 500 students during the day, Loretto Academy was also a boarding school able to lodge 50 pupils. In September 1947, Loretto Academy became the first Catholic high school to admit a black student in Kansas City. In 1966, Loretto Academy sold its facility at Thirty-Ninth Street and Roanoke Road to Calvary Bible College. The school relocated to 12411 Wornall Road, where it remained until closing in 1984.

BISHOP HELMSING AT BISHOP HOGAN HIGH SCHOOL, 1965. Edwin V. O'Hara announced shortly after his installation as bishop of Kansas City in 1939 that he wished for the diocese to construct a new coeducational Catholic high school on Meyer Boulevard between Troost Avenue and Paseo. Bishop Hogan High School began classes on September 10, 1941. The Benedictine Sisters of Mount St. Scholastica in Atchison, Kansas, instructed pupils at Bishop Hogan High. By 1951, there were 560 students enrolled. In 1989, Bishop Hogan High entered into a partnership with Rockhurst College that gave seniors at Hogan access to college classes taught at Rockhurst. In 1999, Bishop Hogan High School became a charter school and was renamed Hogan Preparatory Academy.

ROCKHURST COLLEGE, C. 1970. Having left Kansas City in 1845, the Jesuits returned in 1885 with the intent of establishing a college to serve the area. Nearly 25 years later, after years of planning and raising the necessary funds, Rockhurst College was founded on August 30, 1910. Rockhurst opened its doors to students on September 15, 1914, as construction took four years to complete.

GROUND BREAKING AT ROCKHURST UNIVERSITY, 1993. Academics at Rockhurst were successful from the institution's inception. In 1960, the renowned poet Robert Frost came to speak in the visiting scholar program. Though Rockhurst was originally founded as an all-boys college, in April 1968, the institution announced that it would become coeducational in September 1969. Rockhurst College officially changed its name to Rockhurst University in 1999. Notable alumni include former Kansas City mayor Sly James and George Wendt, known for his role of Norm on the television sitcom *Cheers*.

Redemptorist High School, c. 1960. Our Lady of Perpetual Help Parish School, also known as Redemptorist High School, opened in July 1898 as an all-girls school at Thirty-Fourth Street and Broadway Boulevard. When an arsonist burned down the school, a new facility was built at the corner of Linwood and Wyandotte Streets and opened in February 1925. The new school was built to house 500 grade school and 500 high school pupils. Along with Redemptorist priests, the Sisters of St. Joseph of Carondelet instructed students. In 1940, Redemptorist High School became coeducational. In March 1968, the Diocesan School Board announced that Redemptorist High School would be closing. In 2006, Cristo Rey Kansas City High School was opened by the Sisters of Charity of Leavenworth in the old Redemptorist High building.

GROUND BREAKING AT AVILA COLLEGE, 1964. Avila College was founded in 1916 as the College of St. Teresa. It was renamed in 1963 to highlight the school's patroness, Saint Teresa, who was born in Avila, Spain. In 1940, Avila became a four-year liberal arts institution offering programs in nursing, teaching, and business. Originally located at Fifty-Sixth and Main Streets, Avila moved to its current location at 119th Street and Wornall Road in September 1963. Over $12 million was raised for the construction of Avila at the Wornall campus. Operated by the Sisters of St. Joseph of Carondelet, Avila was a female-only institution until 1952, when the first males enrolled as part-time evening students. In 1966, the first male students were accepted to attend Avila during the day. In September 1969, the first full-time male students were admitted.

Archbishop O'Hara High School Dedication by Bishop Charles H. Helmsing, 1965. The Diocese of Kansas City–St. Joseph launched plans in 1961 for the construction of a new Catholic high school in South Kansas City to be named in honor of former bishop Edwin V. O'Hara. Ground was broken for the new school at Ninety-First Street and James A. Reed Road on June 7, 1964. Archbishop O'Hara High School was dedicated on April 23, 1965, by Cardinal Joseph Ritter of the Archdiocese of St. Louis. Classes began in September 1965. O'Hara High School was unusual for two reasons compared to other Catholic high schools in Kansas City. Firstly, it was coinstructional but not coeducational, meaning that while both boys and girls attended the school, separate classrooms were provided for instruction according to gender. Secondly and most interestingly, the high school produced its own electrical power through the use of natural gas. O'Hara High School closed in 2017.

STUDENT-CADETS AT DE LA SALLE HIGH SCHOOL, C. 1950s. Bishop John J. Hogan invited the Christian Brothers to serve in Kansas City in September 1887 with the understanding that they would establish a school, first at Eighth and Cherry Streets on the campus of Old St. Patrick Parish and later at Twelfth Street near the cathedral. The Christian Brothers founded De La Salle Academy in 1911 at Sixteenth Street and Paseo. Military training was added to De La Salle's curriculum in early 1942 due to the high number of young men being drafted for service in World War II. Because of this, the school became De La Salle Military Academy in 1942. In September 1960, military training was terminated at the school. The Diocesan School Board announced in May 1971 that De La Salle would not be reopening in the fall semester.

GROUND BREAKING FOR DONNELLY HALL AT ST. TERESA ACADEMY, 1940. The Sisters of St. Joseph of Carondelet founded the all-girls St. Teresa Academy in 1866 at Fifty-Sixth and Main Streets in Kansas City. St. Teresa's received its accreditation from the University of Missouri in 1908 and was the first Catholic school to be affiliated with the university and its educational system.

STUDENTS AT ST. TERESA ACADEMY, 1995. St. Teresa Academy became accredited by the North Central Association in 1928. As enrollment increased during the early 20th century, new facilities were needed to better accommodate the student body. The ground breaking for Donnelly Hall on the campus of St. Teresa occurred in 1940. St. Teresa's was distinguished in 1984 with a citation by the National School Recognition Project as one of the Top 60 private schools in the United States.

Class at Our Lady of the Americas, 1966. Our Lady of the Americas School was formed through the consolidation of Sacred Heart Parish School and Cathedral Parish School in 1966. The school operated at the two locations from its amalgamation—at Twenty-Third and Madison Streets (Our Lady of Guadalupe) off of Southwest Boulevard as well as Twenty-Sixth Street (Sacred Heart Parish). Comprised primarily of Hispanic students, particularly Mexican Americans, the majority of the pupils came from Our Lady of Guadalupe Parish. Though lay instructors taught at Our Lady of the Americas beginning in 1966, both the Sisters of St. Joseph and the Sisters of Loretto served as teachers at both locations. However, the Sisters of St. Joseph left the school in 1980, and the Sisters of Loretto followed in 1981. In October 1991, Our Lady of the Americas entered into a cooperative program with Our Lady of Perpetual Help Parish school that took effect in 1992. The school changed its name to Our Lady of Guadalupe School in December 1991.

BLESSING AT ST. PIUS X HIGH SCHOOL, 1995. During the 1950s, the areas of Kansas City north of the Missouri River in Clay and Platte Counties swiftly expanded in population. Discussions began within the then-Diocese of St. Joseph that a new Catholic high school should be built to accommodate the Catholic communities north of the river. The new school developed as St. Pius X High School, and it became the first Catholic high school built in Kansas City since 1940. In 1956, Clay and Platte Counties were incorporated into the newly created Diocese of Kansas City–St. Joseph. On April 28, 1957, Bishop John Cody dedicated the school constructed on Forty-Second Terrace. The high school was finally completed in 1959. In 1987, a life-sized statue of Saint Pius X was dedicated at the high school.

SCIENCE BOWL COMPETITION AT ROCKHURST HIGH, 1985. The founding of Rockhurst High School is intrinsically linked to the establishment and operation of Rockhurst College. Since Rockhurst College's inception in 1910, boys attended a high school on the college campus at Fifty-Second Street and Troost Avenue. However, in 1957, plans emerged for a standalone high school facility away from the college. In 1961, construction began on Rockhurst High School at Ninety-Third Street and State Line Road. Bishop Charles H. Helmsing dedicated the new school on September 30, 1962, with approximately 3,000 people attending the ceremony. Administration of Rockhurst High School separated in 1962 from that of Rockhurst College; the college's president had directly administered the high school for the past 52 years.

Fr. Benedict Justice School Class, 1988. Named in honor of a much-beloved Franciscan priest who served at St. Joseph Parish in Kansas City, Missouri, as well as at Our Lady of Perpetual Help in Kansas City, Kansas, Fr. Benedict Justice School was created in February 1971. The school formed through the combination of the grade schools from St. Vincent's, Holy Name, and Annunciation Parishes. The intent for the formation of Fr. Benedict Justice School was to better serve the educational needs of inner-city schoolchildren, particularly African Americans. Initially, Fr. Benedict Justice School operated at two separation locations: Holy Name and Annunciation. This arrangement lasted until September 1980, when the school moved permanently to Annunciation School. Due to declining attendance, the decision was made to close Father Benedict Justice School in May 1988.

Four

Religious Orders and Lay Organizations

Without the presence of religious orders in western Missouri, it is quite probable that Catholicism would not have taken root in Kansas City. Though the Jesuits had passed through the area as far back as the 17th century, the order's attention turned to bringing the gospel of the Catholic Church to the Native Americans living along the Missouri River. Catholicism was further solidified by the arrival of Jesuit father Nicholas Point and Fr. Peter DeSmet in 1840.

The Jesuits have had a major impact on Catholicism's success in Kansas City, which includes founding multiple parishes like St. Aloysius and St. Francis Xavier. Other religious orders are equally responsible for the growth of the church in Kansas City. The Redemptorist Fathers, the Scalabrinians, the Sisters of St. Joseph of Carondelet, and the Benedictine Sisters of Atchison, Kansas, are just a few of the ordered clergy who have provided education, medical care, and spiritual nourishment to the Catholics of Kansas City.

But the success of the church and its growth cannot be pursued by priests, bishops, and religious orders alone; it also has to come from the common lay people. To this end, lay organizations have been founded comprised of every ethnicity in Kansas City to promote the Catholic Church. For the Germans, it has been groups such as the German Church Building Commission. For the Irish, it has been the Ancient Order of Hibernians and Clan na Gael. The influx of Italians and Sicilians into Kansas City during the 1890s led to the establishment of lay groups like the Italian Intersocial Supreme Council of Kansas City. Likewise, black Catholics and Vietnamese Catholics have supported groups like the Knights of Peter Claver and the Vietnamese Mutual Association.

ITALIAN INTERSOCIAL SUPREME COUNCIL OF KANSAS CITY, C. 1950. During the tenure of Scalabrini father Carlo Delbecchi, Holy Rosary Parish's Italian congregation established the Concilio Supremo Intersociale, or Italian Intersocial Supreme Council of Kansas City in 1917. The council was formed by Vincent Cipolla and Dr. Louis Laurenzana. Like other organizations created by ethnic communities, the council was designed as a benevolent society to distribute money to the poor in the North End, with the funds collected from members' dues. During World War I, the council sent money to Italy to support the poor, displaced, and orphans of the nation. The council, like fellow Holy Rosary organizations such as the Intersocial Committee of St. Francis of Assisi and the Salapurata Club, marched North End streets collecting money and displaying their uniquely embroidered flags. A major holiday for Italian organizations like the council was Columbus Day, when they presented a formal program to reaffirm their patriotism as American citizens along with celebrating the discoveries and achievements of Christopher Columbus.

Rev. John Girst, SJ, at St. Francis Xavier, 1959. It is impossible to discuss the history of Catholicism in Kansas City without mentioning the Society of Jesus (Jesuit) religious order. Indeed, in terms of the establishment of permanent Catholicism in the area, the Jesuits are perhaps the most important religious order. Jesuits arrived in 1827 in what would become Kansas City and primarily focused their work as missionaries to the Native Americans living in the area until 1845. The first recorded sacraments come from the Jesuit missionaries to Kansas City. The Jesuits left in 1845 but returned to found St. Aloysius Parish in 1885. Beyond the founding of St. Aloysius and St. Francis Xavier Parish in 1909, the Jesuits also are chiefly responsible for the establishment of both Rockhurst College/University and Rockhurst High School.

Nun from Sisters of St. Joseph of Carondelet, c. 1970. The Sisters of St. Joseph of Carondelet (CSJ) arrived in Kansas City in 1866 and took up residence at St. Teresa's Academy, which served as their first permanent mission in the city. The order was also invited to teach at Old St. Patrick Parish School beginning in 1872. In 1878, CSJ Sisters were responsible for the instruction of the Annunciation Parish School in the West Bottoms, and they remained at Annunciation until 1883. The Sisters of St. Joseph of Carondelet also began operating the St. Joseph Orphan Home in Kansas City in 1880. By 1950, there were 167 CSJ Sisters serving in the Kansas City area, but this number declined steadily after the changes of Vatican II so that only 74 remained by 1990.

Ancient Order of Hibernians, c. 2000s. The Ancient Order of Hibernians is an Irish Catholic organization founded in New York City in 1836 as a mutual aid society to assist recently arrived Irish immigrants to assimilate into American life and protect their Catholic faith. Padraig Pearse Division No. 1 of Kansas City was formed in 1871 and is Kansas City's oldest continually operational civic organization. Though there is now only one division operating in Kansas City, five existed in the city between 1871 and 1930. The Hibernians purchased the old St. Vincent Parish Church in December 1897 and used the facility as a meeting hall until 1930. The mother parish of the Hibernians in Kansas City is Our Lady of Perpetual Help (Redemptorist). Today, the Hibernians are not only dedicated to the preservation of Catholic faith and Irish culture among Irish Americans but are also involved in scholarships for local Catholic schools.

Father Byrne of the Precious Blood Fathers, 1963. The Society of Precious Blood was founded in Giano, Italy, in 1815 by Saint Gaspar del Bufalo. The motherhouse for the Precious Blood fathers in the United States was established in Peru, Ohio, in 1844 and at Carthegena, Ohio, in 1861. Bishop John J. Hogan invited the order to the Kansas City area in 1874.

Kansas City Province of Precious Blood Fathers, 1991. The Precious Blood fathers opened the Del Bufalo Seminary in September 1963 in Liberty. The Kansas City Province of the Precious Blood community was founded in 1965. The seminary changed its name to Precious Blood Seminary in 1966 but closed in May 1971. The Precious Blood fathers still operate St. James Parish in Kansas City.

Council of Catholic Laity Meeting, c. 1967. In July 1967, Bishop Charles H. Helmsing formed the Council of Catholic Laity to serve as the bishop's principal advisory committee. It was also to serve as a liaison between the laity, clergy, religious orders, and the bishop. The founding of such a council represents the dramatic shift in lay relations within the Catholic Church following the changes of Vatican II. The heightened involvement of the laity in church affairs was a theme during the tenures of both Bishop Helmsing and Bishop Sullivan. By 1977, however, it was increasingly clear that Bishop Sullivan was not using the council as his primary advisory body. The council was disbanded in 1980.

SISTERS OF LORETTO AT LORETTO ACADEMY, 1963. The Sisters of Loretto at the Foot of the Cross were founded in St. Charles, Kentucky, in 1812 and arrived in Kansas City at the invitation of Bishop John J. Hogan and Fr. Thomas F. Lillis in 1889. The Sisters served at Father Lillis's parish of the heavily Irish St. Patrick's on Eighth Street until they left the parish in 1893. The Sisters taught at Our Lady of Good Counsel Parish School from 1907 to 1967. They also operated the parish school of Sacred Heart Parish between 1894 and 1981. The largest educational contribution of the Sisters of Loretto within Kansas City was the founding of Loretto Academy in 1901. The Sisters ran Loretto until its closing in 1984.

Group of Women Belonging to the Cursillo, 1990. The Cursillo was founded on the island of Mallorca, Spain, in 1949 as the Cursillo de Christiandad (Course of Christianity) and began initially as a program to train youth leaders on a pilgrimage to the tomb of Saint James of Campostella. The Cursillo movement came to the United States in 1957 in Waco, Texas, and to Kansas City in November 1962. The Cursillo emphasizes and promotes a sense of vocation within individual members of the laity. The diocese's supporter of the Cursillo in Kansas City was Fr. Fidelis Albrecht, OFM, who had been invited by Bishop Helmsing to begin the Cursillo throughout the city. The Catechetical Center at Eleventh Street and Broadway Boulevard hosted the first English-speaking Cursillo for women in May 1967, with Our Lady of Sorrows Parish hosting the first English-speaking Cursillo for men in December 1969. The first Spanish-language Cursillo for men occurred in November 1979 and for women in March 1980.

Catholic Woman's Club, 1988. Bishop Lillis asked the Catholic women of Kansas City to form the Catholic Woman's Club in 1919. The goal of the club was for the bishop's office and Catholic women to work together to better promote the spiritual well-being of youth within the city as well as to provide for their physical well-being. A subsidiary of the Catholic Woman's Club—the Council for Catholic Women—was formed in 1924 and became associated with the National Council of Catholic Women that same year. Camp Little Flower was operated by the club for nearly 50 years beginning in 1908 until the diocese took over the camp's activities in 1958. Although the club no longer ran the day-to-day operations of Camp Little Flower, it still continued to subsidize the camp until its closing in 1980.

KNIGHTS OF COLUMBUS. The Knights of Columbus were formed in New Haven, Connecticut, in October 1881 and were established in Kansas City in 1900. Meeting at the Baltimore Hotel at Eleventh and Baltimore Streets, Dr. B.H. Szartz and J.H. Walsh convinced the other men in attendance that Kansas City Catholic men should begin organizing councils across the city. The first, No. 527, was established on July 1. On July 14, 1900, Judge William B. Teasdale was elected Kansas City's first grand knight. Because Kansas City was one of the first cities west of the Mississippi River to have a council, the city's Knights directed the initiation ceremonies for other cities such as Topeka in September 1900 and Denver in November 1900.

KNIGHTS OF PETER CLAVER JUNIOR DIVISION MEMBERS, 1975. The Knights of Peter Claver are the largest African American Catholic lay organization in the United States, founded in November 1909 in Mobile, Alabama. Their namesake, Saint Peter Claver, was a Spanish priest who ministered to African slaves brought to the New World. The ladies' auxiliary was formed in 1926. The Knights were established in Kansas City through the formation of Kansas City Council No. 57 on November 7, 1928. The Knights of Peter Claver serve the Catholic Church and provide aid and assistance to others while promoting the social and intellectual welfare of black Catholics.

SISTER WATCHING OVER CHILDREN SWIMMING, C. 1960. The Daughters of Charity of St. Vincent de Paul were formed by Saint Elizabeth Ann Seton in Emmitsburg, Maryland, in 1809. Bishop Hogan invited the order to take over the Kansas City Boys Home, and the Sisters assumed control of the orphanage in May 1897. The Kansas City Sisters became part of the St. Louis Province in 1910. In addition to the operation of the Kansas City Boys Home, the Sisters ran St. Anthony Infants Home between 1909 and 1969 and the Seton Neighborhood Center/ Seton Center beginning in 1969.

GROUND BREAKING OF BISHOP LILLIS HIGH SCHOOL, 1940. With their motherhouse in nearby Atchison, Kansas, the Sisters of St. Benedict have served in Kansas City since their invitation to the diocese in 1891, when Bishop Hogan asked them to operate the school at Our Lady of Sorrows. In 1900, the Sisters were dismissed after the parish pastor requested they direct the choir, which they were not allowed to do. They have worked in other parish schools, diocesan high schools, and parochial schools operated by various religious orders in Kansas City, including De La Salle High, Bishop Lillis High, Bishop Hogan High, Notre Dame de Scion High, and Rockhurst College/ University. They have also served in the parishes of Guardian Angels, St. Michael the Archangel, St. Therese North, St. Peter, Visitation, St. Augustine, and Holy Rosary.

Black Catholic Caucus of Greater Kansas City, 1986. The Black Catholic Caucus of Greater Kansas City was founded in 1977. It represents African American Catholics in the region while working in conjunction with nationally recognized Catholic organizations. It is also committed to the evangelization of black Catholics as well as bringing awareness to social conditions of black Catholics in the inner cities. The caucus promotes these ideals through workshops, speakers, and commemorations that celebrate and reinforce the experience of black Catholics. In September 1985, a citywide celebration of black Catholicism was based at the Cathedral of the Immaculate Conception.

Sr. Anna Kiernan (left) and Sr. Anne Mansfield, 1964. Founded at Immaculate Heart of Mary Parish in Holman, New Mexico, on July 16, 1958, the Society of Our Lady of the Most Holy Trinity (SOLT) arrived in Kansas City in 1964 at the invitation of Bishop Charles H. Helmsing. Founder Fr. James H. Flanagan recognized that the organization had to function as a team that emphasized a Marian-Trinitarian communion along with a missionary passion and the importance of teamwork as a family. Therefore, lay people serve alongside the clergy within SOLT. The first parish within Kansas City was St. James the Greater in 1964. SOLT has also served in Kansas City at Blessed Sacrament, St. Francis Seraph, Annunciation, Holy Trinity, St. Michael the Archangel, St. Aloysius, Guardian Angels, Sacred Heart, and Our Lady of Guadalupe.

Franciscan Friars with Bishop Edwin V. O'Hara, c. 1940s. The Franciscans (OFM) of the Province of St. John the Baptist, based in Cincinnati, came to Kansas City at the invitation of Bishop John J. Hogan in 1890. They served at Our Lady of Sorrows Parish, arriving in 1890 and leaving in 1986. The Franciscans were also responsible for the establishment of St. Monica Parish in 1910; in 1940, it became St. Joseph Parish. The Franciscans left St. Joseph Parish in 1991. OFM friars founded Holy Family Parish in Leeds in 1905 and remained until it closed in 1958. They also operated St. Francis Seraph Parish in Kansas City between 1892 and 1959.

Five

Assisting the Community

Though organized in 1917 out of a need to provide a single direction for the efforts of the different Catholic charitable institutions and societies, Catholic Charities' genesis really begins with the building of the St. Joseph Orphans Asylum. Fr. Bernard Donnelly's attention toward helping the needy in Kansas City began with his experience in the city during the Civil War. The destructive nature of the war in western Missouri, with guerilla warfare, reprisals, evictions, and banishments, left many destitute, particularly children. Father Donnelly began to provide shelter for orphans in his private residence at the cathedral by 1863. The establishment of the St. Joseph Orphans Asylum in 1879 is a direct result of this need. The creation of institutions such as the Kansas City Orphan Boys Home in 1895, the Don Bosco Center in 1940, and Good Shepherd Manor in 1967 are excellent examples of the Catholic Church providing relief, education, and hope for those in need throughout Kansas City.

Yet the church in Kansas City has not just relegated its efforts to assist the spiritual and physical needs of others but has also directed immense energies to social justice for African Americans. In March 1965, following the heed of Dr. Martin Luther King for Christians to aid in the struggle for black civil rights, a large contingent of Catholics from Kansas City traveled to Selma, Alabama, to march against white supremacy. The Diocese of Kansas City–St. Joseph was one of the 44 dioceses out of 150 in the United States representing the Catholic Church's commitment to racial justice. Early in Catholic Kansas City's involvement in the civil rights struggle, Fr. Norm Rotert stated that Catholics had to make a decision. Father Rotert asked "Are we willing to put our lives on the line?" For the Catholics of Kansas City who sojourned to Selma, the answer was an emphatic "yes."

Kansas City Boys Orphan Home, 1953. The Kansas City Boys Orphan Home was incorporated in June 1895. There had been a great number of orphans in Kansas City going back to the 1860s. Fr. Bernard Donnelly took many into his private residence after many children lost their parents due to the chaos wrought by the Civil War. Though St. Anthony Infants Home existed to provide care for orphaned infants, until 1895, there was no home available to children who reached the age of six. After its construction on Westport Road, there were 15 boys living in the Boys Orphan Home by 1897. The Vincentian nuns from the Daughters of Charity of St. Vincent de Paul arrived in Kansas City in 1897 and took over the operation of the boys home in 1899. By 1940, the orphanage was caring for 125 boys per year. The orphanage's name was changed to St. Pius X Boarding School in 1953. The name changed once again in 1971, when it became Marillac Home and School.

Cornerstone Laying of Don Bosco Center, 1940. In 1938, the Holy Name Society from Holy Rosary Parish became concerned that there was no community center for young people in northeast Kansas City. The society met with Bishop O'Hara in October 1939 and recommended the construction of what became the Don Bosco Community Center north of Independence Avenue between Charlotte and Campbell Streets in 1940. It is estimated that 152,641 young people partook of its programs by 1955. In June 1988, the center purchased the entire campus of St. John the Baptist Parish to provide services for refugees and immigrants, including English classes and Hispanic social services. Today, the facility is the Don Bosco Senior Center.

Catholic Community Library, 1944. The Catholic Community Library (CCL) opened in the former residence of Bishop Lillis on East Armour Boulevard in 1944. The books were available to anyone anywhere in the diocese. The CCL loaned its books through the mail, which made it quite extraordinary. The Sisters of Social Service operated the library between 1944 and 1969. At the height of its popularity, nearly 40,000 Kansas Citians and other Catholics of the diocese patronized the CCL, which contained over 25,000 books. The CCL closed in December 1969, with its books donated to schools and hospital libraries across Kansas City.

Dedication of Marillac Center by Bishop Helmsing, 1963. Between 1952 and 1961, the Kansas City Boys Orphan Home/St. Pius X Boarding School, St. Pius X School of Special Education, St. Joseph Orphan Home for Girls, and Children's Home of St. Joseph all merged to become the Marillac Center. The center was named in honor of the cofounder of the Daughters of Charity, Sainte Louise de Marillac. Bishop John Cody recommended that the center place a larger emphasis on special education for young people in Kansas City.

Sr. Teresa Joseph, DC, at Marillac Center, 1964. Constructed on 106th Street in 1962, Marillac rapidly shifted its focus to special education for children with learning disabilities. Children lived at Marillac for several reasons, but in particular, it was home to children who did not adjust to living in the environment of a foster home. Therefore, it was important for the center to provide a nurturing atmosphere for troubled children. In 1983, the Daughters of Charity left Marillac, and in 2004, the Marillac campus moved to its current location in Overland Park, Kansas.

Fr. Daniel Howe (left) and Fr. Richard Saale Marching for Civil Rights, 1968. Like elsewhere in the United States during the 1960s, the cause of civil rights affected the Catholic community in Kansas City. In November 1962, the Catholic Interracial Council was founded in Kansas City as a byproduct of hearing Msgr. Daniel Cantwell speak at Rockhurst College. Monsignor Cantwell was active in the cause of racial justice in the Archdiocese of Chicago. In March 1965, Fr. Norm Rotert, Fr. John Cole, Msgr. Victor Moser, Fr. Rene Guesnier, Fr. Richard Saale, and Sr. Mary Leoline, BVM, all traveled from Kansas City to Selma, Alabama, to participate in the nonviolent protest march for black civil rights called by Dr. Martin Luther King. Besides the clergy, some 40 members of the laity from Kansas City also marched for civil rights in Selma. Following the assassination of Dr. King in 1968, rioting occurred throughout Kansas City, with subsequent marches conducted to express the diocese's grief over King's assassination.

CHANCERY OFFICES, 1940. Between the establishment of St. Francis Regis Parish in the 1830s and 1871, there were no chancery offices in the Diocese of Kansas City. In fact, church business was usually conducted ad hoc wherever Bishop John J. Hogan was at any given time. When the Cathedral of the Immaculate Conception was constructed in 1871, the chancery offices moved to the cathedral basement.

CHANCERY OFFICES AT THIRTY-SIXTH STREET AND GILLHAM ROAD, 1988. In 1893, the chancery offices relocated to wherever the bishop resided. This arrangement continued until 1956, when the chancery was relocated to Thirty-Sixth Street and Gillham Road. A $150,000 addition was built in 1959. In 2011, the chancery moved to the historic New York Life Insurance Building at Ninth and Baltimore Streets in Downtown Kansas City.

St. Joseph Orphan Home for Girls, c. 1950s. The St. Joseph Orphan Home for Girls has its roots in the Civil War, when many orphans found themselves destitute. Fr. Bernard Donnelly worked tirelessly to establish a permanent orphanage for the children of Kansas City, and in May 1879, the cornerstone for the St. Joseph Orphan Asylum was laid. Father Donnelly considered the orphanage the most rewarding project in his priesthood. The girls' home was operated by the Sisters of St. Joseph of Carondelet until 1958, when it was deeded to the Diocese of Kansas City–St. Joseph; it was closed that summer.

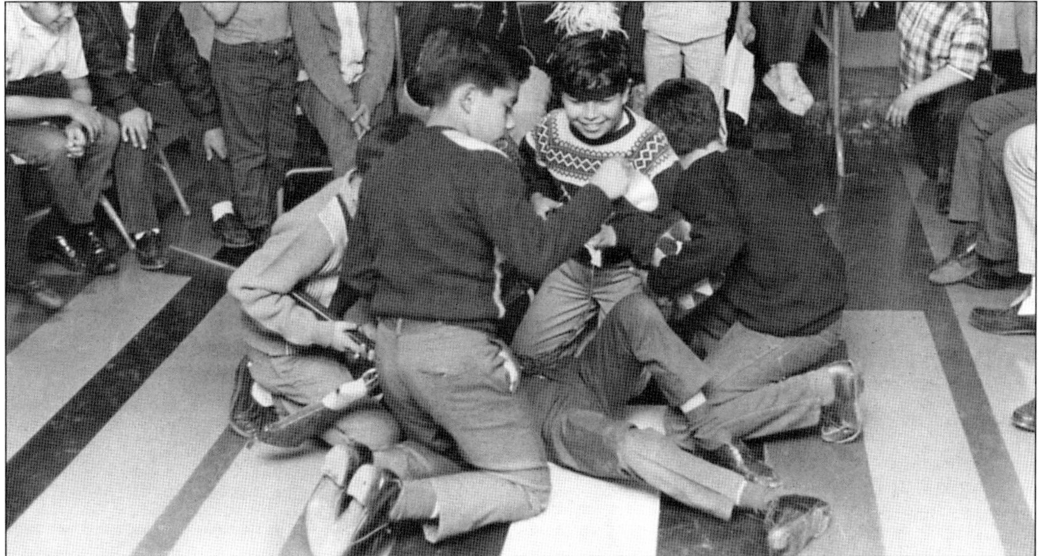

Guadalupe Center Boys Club, 1967. In January 1926, the Guadalupe Center opened to provide clubs for Hispanic youths, primarily Mexican Americans, on the west side of Kansas City. Guadalupe Center also created sports teams, held fiestas, and coordinated other events for young people. Beginning in the 1930s, Guadalupe Center assisted recently arrived Mexicans to assimilate into American life while preserving Mexican folkways and the Spanish language. In 1975, Bishop Helmsing turned over the center's operation to Our Lady of Guadalupe Parish. When the parish closed in February 1991, Guadalupe Center also closed.

ARCHBISHOP O'HARA CATHOLIC YOUTH ORGANIZATION (CYO) MEMORIAL STADIUM, 1980. In 1944, all parishes within Kansas City donated funds for the construction of CYO Stadium at Fifty-First Street and Swope Parkway. It is estimated that 10,000 Kansas City youths and perhaps 100,000 spectators passed through the stadium's facilities. In August 1945, the stadium was dedicated to the servicemen and -women of the US armed forces who served during World War II. To honor Archbishop Edwin V. O'Hara, who was a large supporter of the stadium, the CYO renamed the facility Archbishop O'Hara Memorial Stadium in May 1959. The stadium was sold to the Parks Department of Kansas City after years of poor security and vandalism.

Bishop Lillis Kneeling at Family Tomb, c. 1930. Founded in 1877 by Fr. Bernard Donnelly, Mount Saint Mary Cemetery encompasses 12 city blocks within Kansas City. Many well-known priests and bishops are buried in the cemetery, including Father Donnelly, Bishop John J. Hogan, and Bishop Thomas F. Lillis. Parishioners of Kansas City's first parish, St. John Francis Regis Parish (now the cathedral), who were originally buried on the church grounds of St. John Francis Regis, were disinterred and relocated to Mount Saint Mary in 1877.

Good Shepherd Manor, 1973. Opened in the old clinic of Queen of the World Hospital, Good Shepherd Manor became operational in November 1967. The Brothers of the Good Shepherd established the facility to care for mentally challenged and physically handicapped men aged 16 and older through their lifetime. In 1991, the Brothers of the Good Shepherd left the facility, and the institution became privately owned and operated outside of any religious affiliation.

Catholic Charities at Ward Parkway Shopping Center, 1977. The organization of Catholic Charities in Kansas City begins with the founding of Father Donnelly's orphanage in 1879. Since then, Catholic Charities have expanded immensely to focus on not just the plight of orphans but also to provide spiritual and physical comfort to everyone in need.

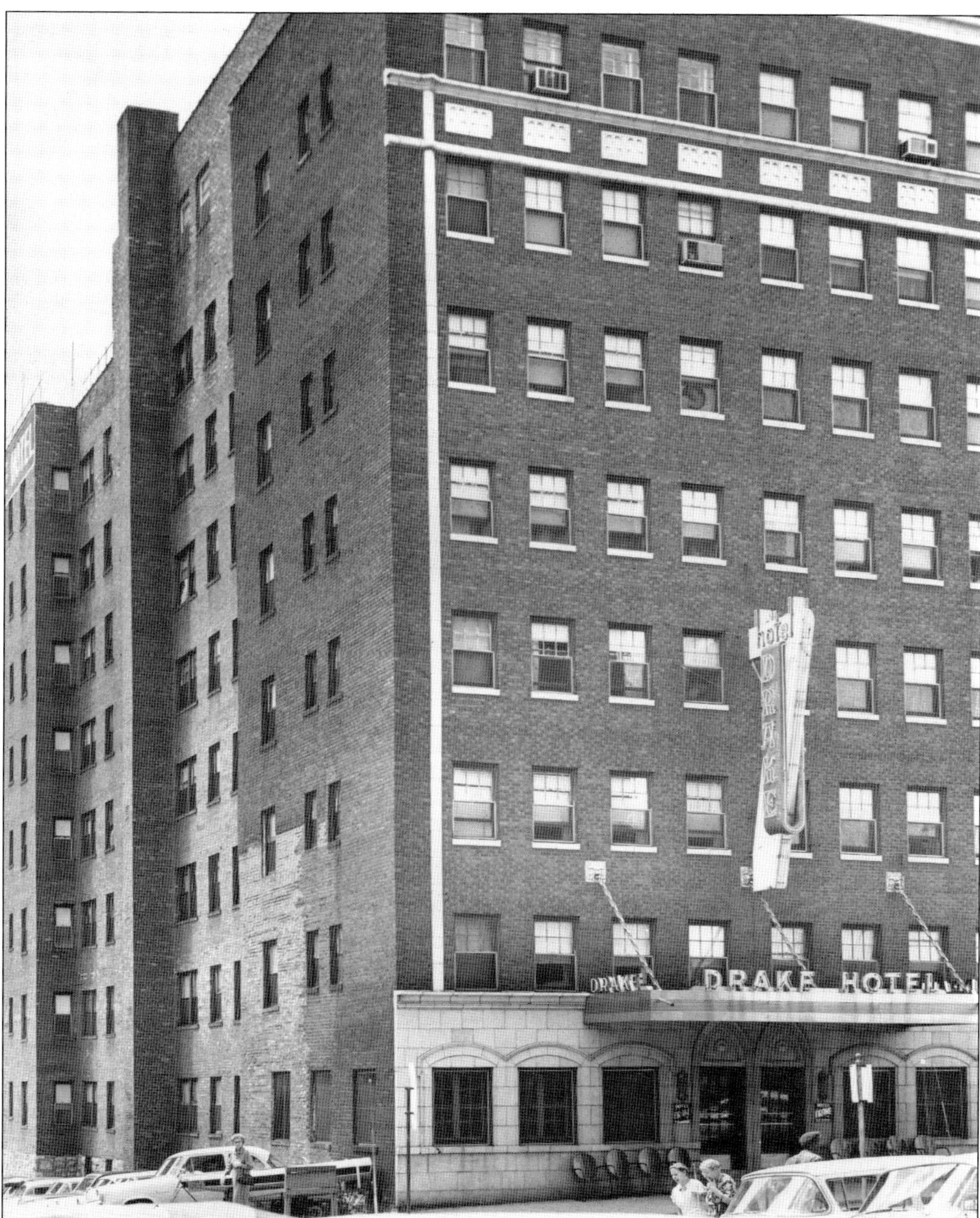

MONTABAUR CLUB, 1959. The Montabaur Club and the Brothers of Mercy Extended Care Facility opened in September 1959. Operating in the former Drake Hotel, on the west side of Locust Street between Tenth and Eleventh Streets, the facility, also known as Mercy Manor, housed retired clergy on its top floor with the rest of the space housing elderly men. In February 1963, the name of the facility was changed to the Montabaur Club by the Diocese of Kansas City–St. Joseph. The Montabaur Club never operated above 55 percent capacity during its time in Kansas City, and the organization was consistently in debt. The Brothers of Mercy, who operated the building, left it in May 1970 and left the diocese in 1976. The Montabaur Club was sold to the Kansas City Housing Authority in February 1971.

Camp Little Flower, 1960. Camp Little Flower operated in Raytown at Eighty-Third Street and Raytown Road beginning in 1930. Prior to that, the camp had been at Winwood Lake in Clay County and then at the former farm of Frank Walsh in Hickman Mills. Camp Little Flower was outside of diocesan control until 1958, when the Department of Catholic Lay Activity assumed management along with the Sisters of Social Services. When the Sisters left the diocese in 1971, the diocese hired a professional lay staff to run the camp. Between 1971 and 1976, the camp witnessed a dramatic uptick, with hundreds of children attending every summer. However, between 1976 and 1979, the camp's attendance declined, and the diocese decided to sell it in 1980. In 1983, the former buildings of Camp Little Flower were destroyed.

Six

Ethnic and Racial Groups of Catholic Kansas City

French Catholics settled along the Missouri River in what later became Kansas City as early as 1819. French families like the Chouteaus and Jarboes made it possible for Catholicism to be established in the area. However, arriving in Kansas City in large numbers following the upheavals of the 1840s and 1850s in Europe, the Irish and the Germans were the first ethnic groups to make Catholicism permanent. The Irish of Kansas City always had a penchant for elaborate celebrations not only of their civic pride but also of their Catholic faith. The *Kansas City Times* reported in 1873 that Irish Catholics belonging to the Ancient Order of Hibernians "marched like soldiers, justly proud of their appearance" through the streets of Kansas City. Like their Irish counterparts, German immigrants were openly proud of their Catholic and ethnic heritage and displayed this pride in drama clubs and Oktoberfest in the city.

The 1890s witnessed the immigration of Italians and Sicilians, who primarily settled north of Independence Avenue in northeast Kansas City. With the arrival of the Italians and Sicilians came Catholic ethnic feasts, celebrations, and traditions. The procession of Our Lady of the Audience and the St. Joseph Tables highlight Catholicism among the city's Italian and Sicilian population.

Catholicism among black Americans in Kansas City began to thrive in 1910 with the establishment of St. Monica Parish at Fifteenth Street and Paseo. Catholicism further took root within the black community as Catholic educational institutions were formed in the inner city. The Black Catholic Caucus and Knights of Peter Claver further reinforced the Catholic Church's central role in the lives of black Kansas Citians.

Numerous waves of immigration of Hispanic Catholics took place in Kansas City from the early 1900s through the 1970s and 1980s. Though Mexican Americans comprised the majority of the Hispanics, Catholics from Central and South America have also settled in Kansas City. The influx of Vietnamese Catholics commencing with the fall of South Vietnam in 1975 represents the latest immigration of nonwhite Catholics into Kansas City.

Our Lady of Good Counsel at St. Patrick's Day Parade, 1984. Irish Catholics began to trickle into the area during the 1830s. The Irish had been persecuted for their Catholic faith under the British for centuries and arrived in the New World to find their situation not much better. Arriving in steady numbers in Kansas City during the 1840s and 1850s, Irish Catholics still experienced anti-Irish bigotry from native-born Protestants.

Gaelic Mass at Redemptorist Parish, 1993. Despite the challenges faced by the Irish in the early years of their arrival, they came to compose an important segment of Kansas City's Catholic population. Many figures in the history of Kansas City Catholicism have had Irish ancestry, including Fr. Bernard Donnelly and five of the seven bishops of the diocese. Kansas City's Irish population, settling in neighborhoods like Kerry Patch near Thirty-Third Street and Broadway Boulevard, is the third largest in the United States behind Buffalo, New York, and Pittsburgh, Pennsylvania.

German Parishioners outside Our Lady of Sorrows Parish, c. 1890. Much like the Irish, German Catholics also came to Kansas City to escape religious persecution during the 1840s. German Catholics initially attended SS. Peter and Paul Parish at Ninth and McGee Streets in 1866. Since many could not speak English, Fr. Bernard Donnelly requested the assistance of Fr. Francis Ruesse to minister at SS. Peter and Paul and hear confession. As the Germans migrated southward in Kansas City during the late 19th century, Our Lady of Sorrows was established in 1890 to serve German-speaking Catholics in Midtown. There were so many German Catholics during the mid- to late 19th century that Bishop Hogan invited the Society of the Precious Blood to minister to the German speakers of the area.

Our Lady of the Audience Procession, 1981. Many of the Sicilians and other Italians who immigrated to Kansas City did so during the 1880s and 1890s in search of work in the railroad industry or as skilled laborers in masonry. The largest group that settled in the North End neighborhood near Columbus Park were Sicilians. By 1929, in fact, 85 percent of all Italian speakers in Kansas City were of Sicilian heritage. With their arrival came Sicilian religious feasts and traditions; one of the most important was the feast of Maria Santissima dell'Udienza, or Our Lady of the Audience. This feast is honored by the Sicilians of Holy Rosary Parish on the last Sunday of May with an outdoor procession held after Mass. Before the statue is returned to the church, there is a traditional shower of flower petals by parishioners.

St. Joseph Table, Holy Rosary Parish, c. 1970. The traditional Sicilian Tavolata of St. Joseph was introduced at Holy Rosary Parish in the late 1880s and continues to be celebrated every March 19, the Feast of St. Joseph. Originally, parishioners prepared a variety of homemade dishes and created elaborate displays in their homes, and parish priests would come and bless individual families' St. Joseph Tables. Because of the lavish displays, the St. Joseph Table was moved into the Holy Rosary Parish Hall in 1950, allowing the creativity of parishioners to be fully exhibited.

Italian and Sicilian Mothers at St. John Bosco Center, c. 1950. The Italian and Sicilian population of Kansas City nearly tripled between 1890 and 1900, increasing from approximately 721 to 2,000. One of the most important developments for these communities was the arrival of Missionaries of St. Charles (Scalabrinians) in 1890. Fr. Ferdinando Santipolo ministered to the Italian and Sicilian population and opened Holy Rosary Parish in 1895.

Black Catholic Parishioners. The early history of black Catholics in Kansas City is fraught with many unknowns. Slaves lived in the area in the early 1800s, owned by French and Spanish Catholics. These slaves were typically considered part of the extended family and were subsequently baptized into the Catholic faith of the white family. Before he became bishop of Kansas City, Fr. John J. Hogan had personally witnessed the cruelty of slavery around Kansas City before the Civil War but kept his opinions private out of fear for his life. Many blacks left the area following the Civil War to migrate west and north for better opportunities. The few who remained did attend Mass alongside whites in parishes such as the cathedral and elsewhere until *Plessy v. Ferguson* in 1896.

Black Parishioners Receiving Communion. Catholicism found increased success among Kansas City's black population beginning in 1910 with the establishment of St. Monica Parish at Fifteenth Street and Paseo. The Franciscan friar assigned to St. Monica, Fr. Cyprian Sauer, searched Kansas City for black Catholics and found only 30. Black Catholics also attended St. Joseph Parish at Nineteenth and Harrison Streets. In 1931, a mission for black Catholics named St. Benedict the Moor was established between Tracy Avenue and Fifth and Sixth Streets. By 1940, so many black parishioners attended St. Monica that three Sunday Masses were required to fulfill the spiritual needs of the community. Despite the dire beginnings, remarkably, by 1991, three thousand registered black Catholics lived in Kansas City.

Redemptorist Parish Festival, c. 2000. Though Kansas City's Hispanic population has for the most part consisted of Mexican Americans, other populations entered into the city well into the 1980s. Since the late 1800s and early 1900s, four separate waves of immigration defined Kansas City's Hispanic population. Beginning in latter half of the 19th century, Mexican migrant workers arrived working on the Santa Fe and Southern Pacific Railroads. A second wave arrived after being displaced by the Mexican Revolution of 1910. The third wave arrived from Mexico and the American Southwest looking for jobs in the war industries during World War I. Finally, a fourth wave of Hispanic immigration took place in the 1970s and 1980s due to conflicts in Nicaragua and El Salvador.

Feast of Our Lady of Guadalupe, c. 1990s. Part of parish life at Our Lady of Guadalupe is the traditional fiesta, first held in August 1926, and the feast day of Our Lady of Guadalupe on December 12. At the 1983 fiesta, an estimated 20,000 people came out to celebrate at Crown Center. It is also estimated that there was a record number of Mexican dishes served to the attendees there: approximately 5,000 burritos, 9,000 enchiladas, 5,000 tamales, and 10,000 tacos. While the feast day of Our Lady of Guadalupe is traditionally held at the parish, the fiesta has been held at a variety of locations across Kansas City ranging from Crown Center to the downtown airport.

VIETNAMESE REFUGEES IN KANSAS CITY, C. 1975. The last major immigration of nonwhite Catholics in Kansas City was the Vietnamese beginning in 1975. At that time, South Vietnam was taken over by communist North Vietnam, and thousands of refugees made their way to Kansas City to avoid persecution. Primarily settling in the Columbus Park area of northeast Kansas City, most attended Holy Rosary Parish at 911 East Missouri Avenue. Catholicism among the recently arrived Vietnamese was extraordinary—90 percent were Catholic. Besides Holy Rosary, many Vietnamese attended St. Francis Seraph Parish at Eighth and Agnes Streets. The Diocese of Kansas City–St. Joseph and its parishes throughout Kansas City gave generously to the refugees, sponsored Vietnamese families, and purchased plane tickets to Kansas City for them. The diocese also established a resettlement office in June 1975 to assist Vietnamese refugees in locating housing.

Celebration of Tet, c. 1980. The Catholic community of Kansas City and the diocese at large also set up job interviews for Vietnamese immigrants as well as English-language classes. The Catholic community center in Kansas City, the Don Bosco Center, was the epicenter of assistance for the Vietnamese community since their arrival in 1975. A successful byproduct of the Don Bosco Center's English courses was that it attracted other non-English speaking Catholics of the city like Hispanics and Filipinos. Ultimately, the Don Bosco Center sponsored 38 Vietnamese families and assisted approximately 319 Vietnamese by November 1975. The formation of the Vietnamese Mutual Association (VMA) in January 1976 further solidified the permanency and success of the Vietnamese community in Kansas City. The VMA was formed in an apartment at Fourth and Tracy Streets and governed by a five-member board who served without salaries.

TET MASS, C. 1980. Arriving alongside their lay brothers and sisters in 1975, Fr. Nguyen Ngoc Thanh and Fr. Phan Duc Dong became the first two Vietnamese priests to minister in Kansas City. As there was not a permanent parish to celebrate Mass for the immigrants, Holy Rosary agreed to host Masses in Vietnamese. The overall effort by the diocese and the Kansas City Catholic community was extraordinary, as approximately 500 Vietnamese refugees were sponsored by 1977. By 1980, the Vietnamese population of Kansas City had grown steadily, and Fr. Joseph Phan Trong Hanh was appointed by Bishop John Sullivan as the first permanent pastor of the Vietnamese Catholic Community. In 1982, the bylaws of the Vietnamese Catholic Community were written, which emphasized a continued strong commitment to the Catholic faith and a joint effort to retain Vietnamese cultural folkways while assimilating into American society.

Vietnamese Boy Praying, c. 1980. The Vietnamese Catholic Community received an instructor for religious education in 1982. Sr. Khiem Tran arrived in the United States, first living in Springfield, Missouri, then moving to Atchison, Kansas, to attend Benedictine College in 1976, where she later took her vows in the Benedictine Sisters of Atchison. She taught religious education courses at Holy Rosary Parish. Though Mass at both Holy Rosary and St. Francis Seraph Parishes was enjoyed by the Vietnamese Catholic Community, the goal had always been to have a parish to completely call their own. When St. Augustine Parish at Seventy-Eighth Street and Paseo closed, the opportunity arose to establish a totally Vietnamese parish. Finally, after many long years, in 1991, the Vietnamese Catholic Community relocated to the former St. Augustine grounds and renamed the parish Church of the Holy Martyrs.